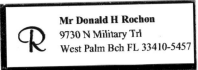

Mr Donald H Rochon
9730 N Military Trl
West Palm Bch FL 33410-5457

P9-DEF-314

The Life of O'Reilly

The Life *of* O'Reilly

*The Amusing Adventures of
a Professional Irish Caddie*

JOHN O'REILLY & IVAN MORRIS

Sleeping Bear Press

For Ben Dunne, Darren Clarke, Paul McGinley, and Philip Walton
who stood by me and helped me get back on my feet after my
serious accident in 1995. Dermot Desmond, J.P. McManus, and John Magnier
for their assistance with my Guide Dogs Charity and other things.
Paul, Peter, and John Kennedy, Jean O'Donnell and staff at Spawell Golf Centre, Dublin
and all the lads in Molloy's Pub, Tallaght, Dublin.

Acknowledgments

I would like to thank my chief motivator, Ivan Morris, who talked me into doing something that had been in the back of my mind for a long time. Ivan was a hard taskmaster but also an inspiration and a pleasure to work with. His encyclopedic knowledge of golf and of those who make their living from it amazes me, especially when you consider that he is an "outsider"—an amateur who was never involved in professional golf in any capacity. He knows his stuff, though.

After Ivan propositioned me successfully, he gave me a tape recorder and showed me how to use it as if he were sitting beside me instead of being 130 miles away. He helped me to organise my thoughts, and then he put them down on paper for my approval. I am glad to say that I am quite pleased with the results.

I would also like to thank Ivan's charming wife, Marie, who gave me a sincere and warm welcome whenever I went to Limerick for one of the business-like but enjoyable head-to-head sessions with Ivan.

Furthermore, he successfully nominated me to be inducted into the Professional Caddies Hall of Fame in America. Being in the Hall of Fame puts me up there with some very famous names in the history of golf: Creamy Carolan, Tip Anderson, Angelo Argea, Jimmy Dickinson, and Alfie Fyles, to name but a few. It is very satisfying to be regarded as a small part of golfing history in this way and I am most grateful for it.

—John O'Reilly

Foreword

Caddies have always had a special place on the European Tour down through the years and John O'Reilly is a very special person. The role of caddie might appear, on the surface, to entail little more than carrying the golfer's bag and, to use an old adage, "Turn up, keep up, and shut up." However that would be to underestimate caddies in general, and John in particular.

I remember our first meeting in Germany many years ago when he was caddying for Peter Townsend. That week, we enjoyed a cup of tea together—the first of many we shared down the years—and I found John extremely engaging company and a wonderful character.

Caddies do tend to be gregarious and colourful and John fits that bill perfectly. He has also been the consummate professional while working. First with Townsend, then during his many years with Des Smith, and more recently with Padraig Harrington before he decided that carrying a 50-pound bag for up to six miles a day was a task for a younger man.

We always hit it off when we met. He clearly enjoyed his work on the Tour and life in general. He always had a good story to tell and many of them are contained in this book. I am delighted that John asked me to write this foreword, and on behalf of the European Tour I would like to wish him every success.

Ken Schofield CBE
Executive Director
European Tour

Table of Contents

Introduction

When my cousin, the late Roland Stafford, telephoned me from Florida to tell me that he was coming to Ireland to play in the 1995 British Seniors Championship at Royal Portrush, he asked me to find him comfortable lodgings and "a good caddie." Little did I realize the chain of events that this simple request would set in motion. I volunteered to caddie for Roland but the offer was spurned.

"You talk too much and over-analyse everything," he said. "Get me a pro caddie who will know his place."

Within a week or two after speaking with Roland, I met fellow Irishman and European Tour player Philip Walton at the J.P. McManus Pro-Am at Limerick Golf Club. Walton had won the English Open a couple of days previously. After I had congratulated him, I told Philip that I was looking for a good, professional caddie. "How would I go about finding one?" I asked.

"Talk to Reilly over there," Walton replied, nodding in the direction of a gray fox of a man standing nearby. That is how I met John O'Reilly, Ireland's most successful and famous caddie. With 25 years of experience working on the European Tour, "Reilly" was perfect for Roland. In fact, "they" were in contention at the halfway stage of the tournament. I wanted to lend my support, so I drove 350 miles through the night so that I could be there for the weekend. Unfortunately, Roland and John didn't win. Afterward, Johnny asked me for a lift back to Dublin. On the way, he told me a series of stories about his soft life and hard times as a professional caddie that had me enthralled.

Obviously, it never occurred to me at the time that I would write John O'Reilly's book. When I wrote my own memoir, *Only Golf Spoken Here: Colourful Memoirs of a Passionate Irish*

Golfer (www.sleepingbearpress.com), I included a chapter about some of my favorite Irish caddies, one of whom was Johnny. I had almost finished *Only Golf* when I accidentally met him for the first time since we'd taken that road trip together. My writing juices were up, and I wanted to keep going, so I asked him if he had any more stories like the ones he had told me five years earlier. He said he had, "and more along with them."

Once we got started, I must say that I have rarely enjoyed anything as much as writing the life story of a man that even the great Spanish golfer Seve Ballesteros refers to as "The Legend."

Ivan Morris
Limerick, Ireland

Reilly the Globetrotter

Remember the old recruiting advertisement, "Join the Navy and see the world"?

Well, I did it my way—a far, far better way, I believe. I became what could be called "an intrepid, globetrotting, European Tour golf caddie."

You could definitely say that mine was an up-and-down existence with never a dull moment. There were many highs and lows, for sure. Most of them caused by the fluctuating fortunes of the golfers I worked for as much as anything I did myself. I would not call it a hard life but it certainly wasn't a soft one, either.

Perhaps before I go any further I should give you a flavour of what can arise if you happen to be the sort of determined, uninhibited world traveller that I became. It was all in the pursuit of an honest day's work and the overriding, sole desire to be on the first tee when my player's name was called. That prerequisite was paramount. I looked on all of the inconvenience incurred and nerve-wracking excitement as a necessary by-product of my duties rather than from any deep-rooted desire for adventure. All I was ever trying to do, like the golfers I worked for, was make a few bob. The bigger the cheque my player won, the more I earned myself (and the more I liked it). But there were many poor days, too. Actually, many times my hardest task was what I had to go through in order to get to the next golf destination. The following is only one example:

At the end of a very successful 1998 season, my "master" and fellow Irishman, Padraig Harrington, qualified to play in the Sarazen World Open near Atlanta in the United States. The late Gene Sarazen may have been one of the greatest golfing legends of all time—he even began his career in golf as a caddie—but to call his tournament a "World Open" was indeed a bit of a cheek.

It was a reasonably good week for my young master and me; I have been in worse places than Atlanta. Harrington played well and made a decent cheque. Consequently, I made a few bob myself and felt flush. Because I had not seen my great friend Fr. Brendan McBride, the golfing priest from Donegal, for sometime and since he was living and working in San Francisco, I had an uncontrollable, sudden urge to pay him a surprise visit. I felt that a couple of days of relaxation in his company would help me recharge body and soul after a long, hard year. Plus I had a personal problem to discuss with him. After all, I was in the same country and who knew when I would be back in America again. I felt that I had plenty of time to do a quick detour out west before I was due to go to New Zealand about 10 days later to help Harrington and Paul McGinley to retain the "World Cup of Golf" for Ireland which "we" had won the year before at Kiawah Island.

I had a wonderful time in San Francisco which is one of the most beautiful places on God's green earth. Fr. Brendan and I talked a lot of golf in between the laughing and the sightseeing, the highlights of which were a tour of the notorious Alcatraz Penitentiary and a marvellous boat trip under the

Golden Gate Bridge. Everything was exactly the way I
remembered it from Burt Lancaster's great movie *The
Birdman of Alcatraz*. Once I saw the prison, I could not
believe that anyone could ever have escaped from such a
fortress. I guess the ingenuity of human beings should never
fail to surprise. I would have loved to have played golf with
Fr. Brendan but since my accident in Spain (which I will tell
you about later) I was unable to do so anymore. I was having
so much fun in 'Frisco that I stayed longer than I should have
and left myself with only 72 hours to get to New Zealand in
time for the World Cup. It was only then, and because I was
under so much pressure, that I got a bright idea. Since I was
halfway to New Zealand already, I thought that I would con-
tact the airline and change my ticket. I expected that this
would be a mere formality. Fr. Brendan said he would drive
me down to Los Angeles so that I could join the plane for the
final long hop to Auckland.

Disastrously, the severest of administrative complications
arose because I had unwisely purchased two tickets before
leaving London. Firstly, a round-trip ticket from London-
Heathrow to Atlanta, and secondly, a separate ticket from
London-Gatwick to Los Angeles and then onward across the
Pacific to New Zealand for the World Cup. When I phoned
my friendly, helpful airline to inquire if what I had in mind
could be arranged at that late stage, to my utter consternation my simple-sounding request was rejected out of hand.

"You must pick up your ticket at Gatwick or else pay a
$2,000 penalty," I was told.

Good grief! You may as well shoot a man as frighten the
life out of him!

"Can I not have somebody bring the ticket out to me?" I
pleaded.

"No," the unsympathetic airline agent said. "You must collect it personally because your passport has to be verified
before you embark."

Why my departure could not have been changed to Los

Angeles and my passport verified there is still a mystery to me. It meant that I now had to reverse engines and fly back to Atlanta, then to Heathrow, catch a train across London to Gatwick, wait several hours, catch a plane back to Atlanta, wait another few hours, and then catch my connection to L.A. as originally planned. Finally back to where I should have started, I waited another three or four hours before at last being on my way on the final 12-hour leg to Auckland. It all added up to 44 hours of nonstop travel, across so many time zones that my mind was frazzled. Only an experienced touring caddie like me could have survived it. Almost anybody else would have been comatose. Not surprisingly, I did not perform at my best that week. I could neither add nor subtract; calculating yardage was beyond me! My footwork was sluggish and I found it tough to keep in step with my master. While on the course it was difficult to stay awake, whereas in bed it was next to impossible to get any shuteye. My whole system was upside down. Padraig Harrington seemed to be amused rather than annoyed. I had already told him it was going to be my last tournament before I retired for good. I felt like a marathon runner who was doggedly determined to finish on his feet, but in my case with a golf bag on his back. After 50 years of caddying, half of them on tour, I had never been sacked or had failed to finish a tournament. I was proud of that record and I had no wish to blot my copybook at this late stage. In all honesty, I think that Harrington himself had mixed feelings about whether to keep me on or not. He enjoyed my company and the way I looked after him, but he was basically telling me with increasing regularity, *You are too fast for me and I am too slow for you.*

There certainly wasn't anything personal involved. We were too close and had had too many good times together for that. In Padraig's mind it was entirely a matter of what he thought would be best for his golf game. That is all that matters to him. He is completely dedicated to that goal and ruthless about achieving it. I had a particularly good relation-

ship with Padraig's father Pat, a Dublin detective, who from
the very beginning was keen to have his son in the charge of
a "wise old bird" who knew the ropes of international travel
and how to avoid the inevitable pitfalls and potholes that
could arise. I took that part of my responsibilities very seriously and firmly believed that my job of "pulling clubs" on
the golf course was secondary to being a "nanny and gopher"
to all of the players that I worked for down through the
years. I also had a good relationship with Padraig's young
bride Caroline, even though as far as I could see she called
most of the shots and made all of the off-course decisions in
that relationship. Caroline was a "Miss Efficiency" par excel-
lence. Padraig simply worked his butt off on the practise
ground, concentrating on his golf and on how he could
improve his scores. That is all he ever thought about, morning, noon, and night. But after three years of touring, he now
knew the ropes and how to get around without needing an
old geezer like me holding his hand.

I am convinced that what finally undermined our partnership is that Harrington's management team, IMG, was simply
looking for a more "business-like" image and wanted a younger,
more photogenic guy at Padraig's side when he was in front
of the TV cameras. I did not fit the image they were trying
to create. I was too old and scruffy-looking, even though I
wore cashmere as expensive as the next guy. Some fellows
look cashmere. I did not.

On balance, it was probably time for me to take life a little
easier. At the age of 60 years my pins were beginning to give
out from all of that walking, not to mention me poor old
back, broken from lugging a wardrobe full of golf gear around
the courses of the world. I had been travelling far away from
home for long enough. All of that globe-trotting was beginning
to wear me down. Besides, my family of six children (aged
between 19 and six years) probably needed their father to be
around the house more often.

I miss the adrenaline of being involved in golfing battles

and I also miss looking forward to the next tournament, which is always going to be better than the last one. But I emphasise it is the anticipation that I miss, not the act of living it. I also miss my buddies, but as most of them have left the Tour themselves by now for one reason or another, that loss is irrelevant. I certainly do not miss all of the waiting around in airports and rail stations. There is a new breed of caddie on tour these days with which I have not got a lot in common. Some of them are university graduates and whizzes at stocks and shares rather than being interested in a flutter on the gee gees (betting on horse races). Nor do they hang around bars or look much like the scruffy lot who worked the Tour when I began. But I want to tell you that most of those old guys were salts of the earth. They would give you the last penny in their pocket if you needed it more than they did. We all pitched in and helped one another, pooling information and resources. We hung around together and travelled together, always taking care that everyone had enough food and at least a roof over his head at night. We shared everything, including our beds when we had to on occasion. Most important of all, we made sure everyone got home safely with a few bob in his pocket, whether they had misbehaved or not. These days the Tour is more serious, more impersonal, and not as much fun as it once was. The money is so vast nowadays that everything has to be more businesslike and organised (even the caddies have their own association with strict rules of conduct and a code of ethics). Nowadays the caddies receive meal vouchers and have a common room, henceforth referred to here as the Caddie Shack, into which they can put their personal things, take shelter or a rest. That facility is of very recent vintage and long overdue. Any caddie with one of the current top guys is far better off than most of the *players* were in my early days. With so much money available, I suppose it is inevitable that golf has become deadly earnest and has attracted a plethora of sharks, scavengers, and hangers-on.

New millennium players pay far too much of their hard-earned money to their so-called managers, who in many cases are little short of being parasites. Players should remember that their office is out on the golf course. That is where they should produce the goods. Thinking about off-course activities too much blunts their ability to perform and a downward spiral begins. It has happened to hundreds of top players—Tony Jacklin being the most outstanding example in my lifetime of allowing himself to be distracted into losing focus when he had the world at his feet. Players become interested in off-course earnings because they think it is easy money and they are greedy. There is no such thing as "easy money." There is always a price to be paid. If the price is one's core ability to play good golf, then that is too high a price to pay. Money is always replaceable but "good form" is not.

Tantrums, Pranks, and High Jinks

It is all very well for the ordinary golf follower to sneer at some of the tales out of school that I am now about to reveal. But I want to preface this chapter by saying that it is a jungle out there on the professional golf tour. There is no place for a caddie or his player to hide; if the cannibals don't get you, the quicksand will. While the thought of either should keep the adrenaline working overtime, there is the other side of the coin, the bloody boredom. The boredom of waiting in airports, in clubhouses, and during the play itself. All that waiting can really gnaw at you. It is the biggest mental hazard that journeymen pros like Des Smyth and Eamon Darcy who are both still out there after 28 hard years of playing and waiting for a living, have to overcome. They must be men of iron will, infinite patience, and total dedication because I know that they are both looking forward to continuing on in the same vein when they hit 50 and become members of the Senior Tour.

Why do they do it? First of all, they really love the game. They also like being out in the fresh air. And it's their job, just like caddying was mine. No matter how badly they might play, there is always the hope that next week will be better, and hitting the jackpot may be just around the corner. All they need for that to happen is to have a hot putter for a few weeks. Every pro is capable of that.

Although I was disappointed at first when Padraig Harrington and I parted company in 1999, I have no regrets looking back. Without quite realising it at the time, I was on a treadmill that had to stop sometime. Once it did stop, I was ready to get off and end my wandering for good. Enough was enough; I soon resolved that I would never go back. Life on tour these days, for both caddie and player, is a young man's game and it is no place for a 60-year-old.

One of the great secrets of being a good caddie is having the ability to read all the players' moods whether you are working for them or not. Knowing when to laugh or cry, speak or remain silent, get involved or look the other way is vital. Golf can do strange things to perfectly nice, normal people. I have seen good minds bent, burnt, and twisted by the cruelty of the game. Those who can remain relaxed and are able to see the funny side of golf definitely last longer. Whether they are laughing at themselves or at somebody else does not really matter. Having a bit of fun and laughter is not only good for every golfing soul, it can help the performance as well. I have always seen it as a big part of my job to try to help my player remain relaxed and not get too uptight. It may explain why in 25 years of full-time caddying on tour that I had only three regular bosses: Peter Townsend (7 years), Des Smyth (14 years) and Padraig Harrington (3 years). I think they appreciated my efforts to help their mental well-being. At least I hope so.

Over the years I caddied for many other professionals apart from the main three mentioned, but they were all casual appointments for no longer than a week at a time. A change is as good as a rest and it sharpened me up, stopped me from getting sloppy, and made me appreciate the guy who was my

The European Professional Golf Tour can be a bit of a circus sometimes and if you saw the antics of Frank Nobilo at Crans sur Sierre, Switzerland some years ago, you would have thought that he was one of the clowns. Mind you, Frank was not being intentionally funny. Only later did he see the humour of his antics.

"Crans Montana" (as we caddies like to call this exclusive alpine retreat) is home to the European Masters. Its first hole is a short, very reachable par 5. Quite surprisingly, Frank sliced his opening drive into the trees. Forced to hack it out backward, he put his next shot into a greenside bunker. He barely extricated himself from the sand and then took four horrible putts to hole out. A bloody snowman (8)! That was appropriate enough considering we were in the Swiss Alps, but the normally mild-mannered Frank hardly thought so at the time. Saying nothing and showing no visible emotion whatsoever, he walked onto the second tee where his caddie had foolishly and carelessly left temptation lying around in the form of Frank's large blue Mizuno golf bag. I could also see that Frank was looking around and made a quick survey to see if anybody was watching him. Thinking the coast was clear, he aimed a strong kick at the base of his dormant, defenceless golf bag. To his consternation and my amusement his foot went right through the light plastic bottom. If the offending foot could have been withdrawn quickly, hardly anyone would have seen his display of petulance. But his studs (spikes) got caught inside the bag and he could not get his foot free. The more he struggled, the more his clubs began spilling out and scattering all over the tee, creating an enormous racket and bringing about the attention he had wished to avoid in the first place. It was like a scene you would see in a movie like "Caddie Shack." We were all doubled up, laughing at him. Suddenly he stopped, looked at us, turned beet-red with embarrassment, and then joined in the laughter. His caddie had to rush off and find a black refuse sack to act as a piecemeal repair job, so that the round could be completed without depositing Frank's clubs all over the Swiss mountains. Frank played beautifully after the mishap and succeeded in finishing the round under par, which only proves that laughter is often the best medicine. Whenever I have bumped into him subsequently, he never fails to mention that incident as if it were a major watershed in his career. And we laugh about it once more.

******

One of the most hated men on tour (by the caddies) was the late Vinny Baker from South Africa. He was a very mean man. He gave every one of his caddies an unnecessarily hard and unprofitable time. Bad as he was, however, Vinny did not deserve the violent death he met in one of the jungles of Africa some years ago. He was fishing at a lake and was jumped on by two guys who robbed and killed him. Believe me, there were occasions when some of his caddies may have felt like doing something similar. But, of course, it was only the beer talking. There was a classic caddie-style revenge on Vinny in Sweden one year. Sweden is a terrible place for travelling caddies because it is so expensive. We could barely afford to eat (or more importantly, have a beer).

Early in the week we were sitting in the hotel lobby doing the usual caddie thing—waiting—when Vinny walked up to the reception desk.

"May I have my room key, please?"

"Certainly, sir. Number 222, is it not?"

"Yes."

Well, that number hit the bull's eye because it was easy to remember. For the rest of the week all the caddies wined and dined at the expense of Room 222. We had a ball!

At week's end after settling our own bills before departure, we hung around to watch the fun and games. Vinny's bill was about 20 feet long. He went ballistic. The hotel staff was

unmoved. He finally realised he had been hit by a caddie
revenge tactic and there was nothing he could do but pay up
and learn an expensive lesson.

******

    Some stories require me to hide the identity of the guilty
for obvious reasons. Players come and players go on the Tour.
Some who were with us for only a short time made unforget-
table impacts. One such a chap was "Senor Q," a Spaniard
whom we called "The Tasmanian Devil." This guy was unbelievable, capable of anything.
    Smythie was paired with him in Sardinia the year that
there was a shortage of caddies. Like many players, Senor Q
pulled his bag on a trolley that week. At one of the short
holes, which played over water, his ball hit onto the front of
the green but it screwed back into the lake. Three times in
rapid succession it happened. Nobody laughed because it was
too dangerous. Finally, pulling his trolley behind him, he took
off toward the green. Ignoring the fact that the lake was
between the tee and the green, into the water he went, trolley
and all. That lake was noted for its poisonous snakes and God
knows what else, but the inhabitants no doubt took one look
at the scowl on the Tasmanian Devil's face and hid under the
nearest rock. Up to his chest the water rose, but he pressed
on and on before eventually exiting on the opposite side.
Naturally, his golf bag was full of water (who knows, maybe a
fish or snake or two might have been in there as well). He proceeded to drop a ball, took out a dripping club and chipped
onto the putting surface. Once on the green himself, he
started to circle his golf ball, speaking softly at first but gradually working himself up into a screaming frenzy. His finale and
coup de grace was to begin spitting at the offending ball.
Nobody dared to say anything. All of us were petrified, so we
looked the other way. We continued the round in a stony, self-

conscious silence, certain in the knowledge that if anybody said the wrong thing they could have been attacked on the spot.

On the last hole, Q's ball ended up in a greenside trap. He was right up against a steep wall with absolutely no chance of escaping. One, two, three shots were expended before the ball finally struggled free.

"Better watch out lads," I whispered, anticipating what I thought might happen next. But Q did not do exactly what I was expecting. Very slowly, calmly, and deliberately he exited the trap and carefully put away his golf club. Then, because he did not have a caddie, he returned to the trap, picked up a rake, and commenced an exemplary tidying up operation. When everything was restored nice and neat he suddenly wheeled around and around like an Olympic hammer thrower, and threw the rake world-record distance back up the fairway.

There was a huge cheer from the balcony of the clubhouse where the players who had finished before us were lounging around. Senor Q looked up at them, smiled broadly, and made a deep bow.

******

There was also a French pro we called Monsieur T. My pal Alex, who always wore a suit and Trilby hat to work, used to caddie for him. It was dangerous work because I swear that anytime Alex did something wrong such as give a slightly incorrect yardage, Monsieur T would slap him! One day they were on the practise ground (this was back when the players had to use their own practise balls) with Alex well away and waiting to shag the balls when they landed. Unfortunately, Alex was facing into the sun and could not see where the balls were going. Unbeknownst to him, T was hitting the balls 50 yards over Alex's head into a forest. In all, about 50 balls were lost. When Alex was called back to base and T saw how few balls had been recovered, he actually punched poor Alex and knocked him out stone-cold! It won't surprise you to learn that it brought the partnership to an abrupt end.

******

Back in my early days as a caddie, the pros played for "chicken feed" compared with what is offered today. You can only imagine what us caddies earned. We had to live on our wits to survive.

Paris has always been an expensive city to visit. It was especially difficult if you were short of money. My colleague Scotty Gilmour, however, was of the philosophy that you should still have the best. One time five of us caddies found ourselves in a casino that had a swanky restaurant three stories above. After losing the little bit of money we had on the "wheel of fortune" and blackjack, we consoled ourselves by going upstairs and having the very best of food and wine. It was first-class dining all the way. We certainly enjoyed it, but we also did not have the wherewithal to pay for it. Therefore, we decided unanimously that we would beat the cheque!

One by one, the guys excused themselves and nonchalantly slipped away from the table. Anticipating the situation, I had brought an old unwanted jacket just in case I needed to make my escape. So I called our waiter over and politely asked him to keep on eye on my jacket because I had to go downstairs to make an urgent phone call.

"Oui, Monsieur, pas de probleme," says the waiter with a bow.

Poof! I was out of there—gone. As usual "The Professor" (another one of the caddies) was the last to leave. He would never budge while there was even an eggcup of wine left. The eejit forgot we were three stories up and decided that he would make his escape by jumping out the window. Fortunately or unfortunately, depending on your point of view, "The Prof" could not get the damn window open and he was nabbed.

Now we were all in trouble. The gendarmes were called and we all ended up in the local police station trying to explain ourselves. We didn't have a sou between us, so Scotty had to call Tony Jacklin. He came, paid the bill, and bailed us out. At the end of the week, Jacklin docked Scotty's wages and he spent months trying to get us to pay him back. I told him there was "no way" that was I paying.

"It was all the Professor's fault," I said. "He's the one that got caught. If anyone should pay, it's him."

******

When Padraig Harrington signed with IMG, he was given a whole wardrobe of new clothes including a range of fabulous cashmere sweaters. The first day he wore one it poured rain. When we had completed our round, he took off the sweater, handed it to me and asked me to put in the drying room. I thought I could do better than that. I found two hair dryers and I put them up the sleeves, turned them on full blast and went away to do something else. When I came back, Matthew Byrne, who caddied for Christy O'Connor Jr. in the Ryder Cup said to me, "I think I smell something burning!"

It was Padraig's cashmere. One of the sleeves was ruined. I stood there looking at it in unbelieving shock. "What am I going to say to Padraig?" All the caddies were cracking up, falling about, laughing at me. Caddies enjoy seeing one of their own in trouble.

"Here, give it to me," said Blackie, a real joker of a Scottish caddie. Taking a scissors, he ceremoniously cut off the damaged sleeve! "Now," he declared, "tell Harrington to send the bleeping sweater to 'The Fugitive!'"

Padraig only laughed when I owned up and told him the whole story. There were many more free cashmere sweaters to be had.

******

One day I was at Killarney Golf Club. Tony Coveney, the long-serving head professional, called me into his emporium and asked me if I would like a job caddying for two Japanese visitors. He said that he had just kitted them out from head to toe and that they appeared to be wealthy and that they would pay me well. I agreed to caddie for them but I had no idea what I was letting myself in for. Those two could not speak a word of English and had never been on a golf course before in their lives. Like many Japanese "golfers," their golf was confined to hitting balls at multistoried driving ranges. One of them was the President and the other was the Captain of the Hopeless Golfers' Society. Believe me, we were out there for half the day. I tried my best to coach them and steer them around but they were, indeed, hopeless. When we finally finished, I doubled my asking price, told their interpreter what it was, and got it without a demur. Obviously they were pleased with my efforts because the interpreter asked me if I would organise a car and drive them to Ballybunion the next day and caddie for them there as well. A favourable deal was struck and I agreed.

Arriving at Ballybunion, the late, great Sean Walsh, one of the most genial and wisest of club managers, greeted us. "Where did you come from, Reilly?" he asked.

I explained that I was there to caddie for a pair of Japanese.

"I wish you the best of luck," Sean said. "You will not be in before the dark."

"That's what *you* think," says I.

Our tee time arrived and, of course, my two charges hit their first tee shots straight into the graveyard on the right of the first hole. In fairness, they would not have been the first to do this because the beloved departed in that cemetery get no peace at all from being bombarded by errant golf balls, morning 'till night. (I understand that even the great Jack Nicklaus has put a ball in there.)

At the second hole, one guy put his ball into the deep pot bunker beside the green. In the guise of it being a teaching demonstration, I got in there myself and played the shot out for him. I knew that we would be there yet if my friend had tried to play the shot.

The tenth tee is right beside the second green. As there was nobody on it or on the ninth hole, I directed the two lads over to it and we plumbed our way around to the sixteenth green. The geography of the course is such that at this point the seventeenth hole is hidden from view and the clubhouse is clearly visible, so I was able to steer my boys back to the clubhouse. A day's work done in record time. Walsh was startled when he saw us coming in so soon.

"Finished already?" he asked. "That must be a speed record for getting around Ballybunion. "How did you manage it?"

My Japanese friends didn't understand what Sean was asking and I didn't enlighten them. The interpreter paid me (including a big tip) and everybody was happy. Later, Sean asked me again how we finished so quickly. "C'mon, O'Reilly, how many holes did they really play?"

I gave him a wink but left him in the dark.

******

I once caddied for a French guy named Patrick Cotton in the Hennessy Cup at The Belfry. The "Hennessy" was a kind of "Ryder Cup" style series of team matches between Great Britain, Ireland, and Europe. I cannot remember how I ended up with a Frenchman but it was the cause of me having my easiest week ever.

The first morning Cotton was drawn to play Brian Barnes, the big pipe-smoking Englishman. Barnesy was at the height of his powers at the time and he gave Cotton a terrible drubbing. A dog licence, in fact: 7/6.

After that, Cotton was dropped from the action and was never selected to play again. Not only did he not practise, he never appeared again. Which meant that all I had to do was hang around and wait to be paid. I heard later that Cotton had met up with a member of the fairer sex and that they had spent all of their time together "indoors." It was fine by me. I'd relaxed and enjoyed myself. At the end of the week when it was time to be paid, Cotton pulled out a wad of 50-pound notes the likes of which I had never seen before. He counted out 10 of them and handed them to me. I had originally asked for only £300, so both of us were obviously happy with that week's work.

******

Des Smyth once beat the great Spanish player, José Maria Olazabal, in a match-play event at Chepstow in Wales. When we came into the locker room Ollie was bashing the door of his locker with his shoes and shouting in Spanish. I did not have a clue as to what he was saying but it was obvious he wasn't very pleased.

"What's wrong with you, Ollie?" I asked him. "It is only a lousy golf match."

"Reilly, how can a guy who is never on the fairway all day long beat me?"

"I suppose he was just a better chipper and putter than you," I replied.

Ollie smiled, calmed down, and actually agreed that that was indeed the reason why he lost the match. It speaks volumes for the short-game skills of Smythie if an acknowledged short-game maestro like Olazabal took that statement to heart and gave it full respect.

******

Howard Clark is now a happy man. Like David Feherty, he no longer has to flagellate himself playing tournament golf in order to earn a crust. He has found a handy job for himself as a roving on-course golf reporter and analyst, commentating on Sky Television. During his playing days, I never saw anyone get more nervous and uptight than "Clarkie." He could be put off his stroke by the slightest movement or noise and it was nerve-wracking being in the same group with him. Everybody felt that they had to walk on eggshells, almost afraid to breathe. Clarkie used to come off the course completely strung out and unable to speak, which would not be much use to him in his new career.

Away from the course Clarkie is a really nice guy, but on it he was as jumpy as a bag full of cats. One day I saw him sitting in the locker room after a poor round, so shattered he was unable to take off his golf shoes. I sat down and began to help him.

"You know, Reilly, it is only when I put on my golf shoes that I get like this," he said.

"Well, why don't you play in "trainers" then?" I asked, referring to running shoes or workout shoes.

He laughed and said that that was a very funny comment. Then he said that he never should have said anything to me in the first place.

Another TV pundit with a suspect golfing temperament is Ken Brown. Perhaps guys who think deeply about the game put themselves under too much pressure and they crack from time to time. Their brains are not challenged enough during a slow round of golf. To be honest, every round of golf that Ken played was slow, which gave him too much time to think. He was a formidable player but sometimes he could become very ratty with himself and those around him. He fell out with his local, inexperienced caddie at Haggs Castle (near Glasgow) on one famous occasion and banished his helper on the fifteenth tee. Brown, ever the showman, put on the caddie's bib, shouldered his golf bag, and played in without any assistant beside him. I am no psychiatrist, but I do know from observation and bitter experience that it does a player absolutely no good to blame his caddie for anything that might go wrong—

whether it is really the caddie's fault or not. It is how a player gets over the unexpected piece of bad luck, bad bounce, or adversity that will decide how good he is under pressure. Some are a lot better at doing this than others.

******

When a group of grown men get together away from home and in a holiday atmosphere, a bit of juvenile behaviour can sometimes take place. Such was the result when a number of us were housed together in an apartment in Valderrama, Spain, during the Tour championship some years ago. Looking back, I'd have to say that things probably went a bit too far.

A very good friend of mine from Newry, Co. Down, Jerry Mynes, who now lives on the island of Jersey, was the instigator. It all started when Jerry barricaded Philip Walton in the apartment he was staying in after he had gone to bed early because he had an early tee time. The rest of us went out for the night and forgot about his predicament. The next morning, "Waltz" could not get out of his room. Eventually, he climbed out through a window onto the veranda and made his exit via the apartment next door. He did not miss his tee time but understandably he was not very pleased.

Waltz was sure that I was the one who locked him in his room. So the next morning when I got up and went for a shave, I found that my shaving kit bag was full of water and everything inside was completely ruined. I knew Waltz had done it but I played a waiting game before retaliating. On the Sunday Waltz was due to fly to Japan, his caddie, Ray Lachford, had left all of Philip's cases sitting in the hotel hallway waiting for the taxi to call and take them to the airport. When his back was turned I took one of the cases and filled it with water. When Ray tried to lift the case, he said to Waltz, "What have you got in here? It is as heavy as lead!"

By the time they got to Japan, all the water had drained away but the clothes inside were ruined. I thought it was funny at the time, but I don't anymore. However, I'm happy that Jerry Mynes was finally identified as the culprit.

Mynes was a menace on that trip. He tried to get me, too, but I saw what he was up to and turned the tables on him. Sitting at the bar, I saw in a mirror that Jerry was putting a large rock into my grip bag, which was sitting on the patio just outside a French window. I did not attempt to lift the rock-filled bag myself. Instead, I made a point of calling a porter. I then had the poor fellow carry the bag up six flights to Jerry's room and together we lifted the rock into his bed, along with about a dozen empty bottles and cans. When Jerry came home that night, exhausted after another lively night out, he jumped into bed and nearly broke his foot. When I heard all the shrieking and shouting coming from his room, I had a right good laugh.

******

We were having a meal in a Chinese restaurant near the Belfry one evening. I ordered hot-and-sour soup and went to the bathroom to wash my hands. When I came back to the table my soup had already arrived. I'm telling you, it was the hottest soup I ever tasted! I was calling for water by the bucketful all night long and gulping it down, but to no avail. The soup sure had me on fire. Apparently, Waltz had shaken some hot Tabasco sauce into the soup while I was in the bathroom.

The next day my insides nearly fell out all over the golf course. I was in and out of the bushes all day long. Smythie's concentration was inevitably disturbed and he was not a bit pleased. Later he gave Waltz a terrible dressing-down over it.

I had my revenge a few weeks later at Cannes. Waltz and I were walking down the pier looking at the magnificent, expensive boats that were moored there. I mentioned that I would love some ice cream.

"Come on," says Waltz. "It is my treat."

At the ice cream store, I selected the most expensive sundae I could find and lapped it up like a puppy.

"Do you know how much that ice cream cost?" Waltz asked as he watched me devour it. "Fifteen quid!"

"Well," says I. "That squares us for what you did to my soup back at the Belfry!"

We both laughed. In spite of the awful, childish things that we did to each other we have always managed to remain the best of friends.

******

Tommy Ward, Christy O'Connor Jr.'s caddie, and I were friendly with an Irish dentist named Malachy Egan who lived in a small town near Sandwich in the south of England. He told us that when the Open came to Royal St. George's nearby, we could sleep in the attic area of his surgery rooms. He rigged up camp beds for us and showed us the geography of the place but forgot to give us a key. Believe it or not, this place needed a key to get in and one to get out, too.

When we rose in the morning we were locked in and could not get out to go to work. Apparently, the cleaning lady had been in at the crack of dawn performing her chores. She did not know that we were there, and had locked all the doors behind her before she left. In order to get to work, we had no choice but to go out through the skylight, onto the roof, and climb down from there. One of the neighbours saw us on the roof, jumped to the reasonable conclusion that we were burglars, and the police were called. Before we could hit terra firma, the police had surrounded the place. It was only when Malachy came along to vouch for us that we were let off the hook by the long arm of the law. It was the talk of the Open the following morning when the story made headlines in the

British tabloids, much to everybody's amusement.

******

On one occasion an ultrarich American amateur gave me a tip of £1 after I had run myself ragged looking after him. Once again I had been misled by the caddie intelligence system when I was reliably informed that this guy was one of the richest people in the whole of the United States. Well, I can tell you that the reason why some people are so rich is because they spend so little. The American had some excuse because he was using a dreaded electric buggy and I was not actually his official caddie. I more or less inflicted my services upon him when he was drawn to play in Smythie's pro-am group. But a mangy £1 after all I did for him? When he was dispensing his largesse he gave me a tip on one of his horses, which he told me was running in the Epsom Derby a few days later.

"Get your money down," he told me, "he's a sure thing."

Oh, how many times have I fallen for such bum advice?! I decided to put the lousy £1 on the nag but it finished a bad fourth. I suppose that I was lucky it was only a £1 that he gave me. It could have been a lot more and I would have been an even bigger sucker.

******

Smythie was playing in the British PGA championship at Lytham. He was in contention all the way but it was Howard Clark's day and he ended up winning it. During the final round there was a guy in our gallery who was becoming overly excited and a nuisance. He must have considered himself to be some expert because he kept telling Smythie to do this, that, and the other on every tee box. We eventually became fed up with him when he actually walked out onto a tee box at one stage, all wound up and full of misplaced enthusiasm. Professional golfers do not need that sort of thing. They like to be left alone to plot their way from A to B around the course, depending on the putter to create the fireworks.

"Get rid of your man, for (bleep) sake!" Smythie said at last. That was all I needed. I confronted the guy and blistered him with the bluest language I could muster. He stood there blinking at me in a complete state of shock. Finally he slunk away and disappeared into the crowd, never to bother us again. Later in the members' locker room I noticed him changing his clothes.

Uh-oh, I thought to myself. *He must be a Lytham member!* Then it was my turn to be shocked. He began putting on his "dog collar" and red colours of a cardinal of the church. It was only then that I realised that the spectator was actually Cardinal Basil Hume, the Primate of all England!

I nudged Smythie. He nearly collapsed laughing. He told me that I had better go over and apologise to him for my language. When I did, the Cardinal only smiled and said that I was right to get rid of him. He had not realised that he was making a nuisance of himself and not to worry about the language—he had heard it all before. He told me he was a great fan of all the Irish golfers and was always hoping that one of them would win.

"I just let my enthusiasm for the game get the better of me sometimes," he admitted.

He could not have been kinder. It was my turn to be embarrassed. Smythie, of course, thought the whole thing was a scream.

******

At the Dubai Classic in 1989, I was fortunate to meet the well-known racehorse owner Sheikh Mohammed (which I'll tell you about later). The following year, I saw him again at the Curragh Racetrack in the centre of Ireland. I was at the races with my buddy Jack Kelly, a bricklayer. When I spotted the sheikh surrounded by his usual retinue. I said to Jack, "I've met the sheikh, you know. I wonder if he'd remember me."

"G'way oura that," Jack said with a big snort. "No chance." Clearly he did not believe me. However, I *have* met some of the richest and most powerful people in the world from time to time and I can tell you one thing about them: they all have terrific memories for names and faces. So, I told Jack to watch me and I sidled up as close as I could to the sheikh, hoping that he would notice me. Like trying to catch a fish, I knew I could have spooked him if I went too close. I simply made sure that he would see me. Very soon I knew I had him "interested" and that he was trying to place me. Perhaps he thought I was another owner. Hah! Anyway, after a couple of minutes, he says to me, "Didn't I meet you in Dubai last year?"

We shook hands and had another friendly chat. He really loves his horses and is such a normal, down-to-earth chap that it is hard for me to believe he is who he is. Kelly was flabbergasted and could not wait to get back to Molloy's Bar in Tallaght Square to tell all our buddies that I really did know Sheikh Mohammed.

******

After completing the Dubai Classic, the "circus"—as we liked to call it—moved a short distance across the desert to Doha for the Qatar Masters. Doha has a much stricter Muslim regime than Dubai so there are far less foreign influences on the orthodox Arab culture. That means one thing above all others: no bars in sight. To their cost, the English have always undervalued the fact that the Irish have managed to penetrate every corner of the globe. The first time I was in Doha, some of the English caddies thought they would have a bit of fun at my expense and challenged me to suss out the local watering holes by dispatching me to find the local "Irish Bar."

I went downtown on my own to do a bit of window-shopping, but in the back of my mind I was still hoping that by some miraculous means I might find an illicit shibeen somewhere. As I was walking along the main street I heard my name being called. When I turned around, I saw my jockey friend George McGrath. I knew that he would know the local territory inside out, so I told him I was gasping for a pint and asked him if he could direct me to the nearest pub. He said that he could do better than that and would take me to it. I got into his car and we drove a couple of miles out of town to a brand new housing development that appeared to have sprung straight out of the desert. George pulled up in front of an ordinary-looking, semidetached residence and knocked at the door. We were immediately ushered inside, almost as if the owner had been expecting us. We were taken down some steps into a kind of underground garage. There, beyond belief, I found myself in a well-stocked, appropriately decorated, genuine Irish Bar!

It turned out that there were a large number of British and Irish engineers, doctors, nurses, and pilots working in the area and they brought back as much beer and spirits as allowed when they returned from trips outside "the dry zone" to stock their little "home away from home." Apparently the exiles preferred to have a drink in the special atmosphere of their private bar than in their own homes. I asked the owner-caretaker if I could bring along some of the golfers and caddies the following evening to see that it was not a mirage. Permission was generously granted and the legend of Johnny Reilly grew another notch.

******

One of my greatest scams at beating "the system" (and one

that I am most proud of) is putting one over on the R&A blazers at St. Andrews, and a certain Mr. Keith Mackenzie in particular. Mackenzie was the Ayatollah and Boss Man of the R&A before Michael Bonnallack and he simply hated caddies. He detested us, could not stand the sight of us, and he gave us all a terribly hard time. He was forever shooing us away from the front of the clubhouse as if we were school children. He did not want us congregating there after completing our duties, blocking the view of the members inside. In fact, he probably did not want us to be there at all. He seemed to resent the air we breathed.

One day, for a bit of diversion, I announced to a group of players and caddies who were standing on the steps beside the 18th green that I would bet anybody £5 that I could get inside and buy myself a drink at the members' bar.

"Impossible!" I was told in unison. "Not a chance."

Those were magic words to me. Hugh Baiocchi, the fine South African player who is now on the U.S. Seniors' Tour, handed me a fiver and said, "Okay, Reilly let's see you get yourself a drink in there."

I went around to the back of the clubhouse, entered through the locker rooms, which I was entitled to do, and went up to the door of the Members' bar, which I was not. At that point I was stopped in my tracks. The young security man would not budge. I took off my watch and said to him that I was anxious to get away for a bit of grub but I had to give my Smythie his watch first.

"Sorry, sirr," the guard said, "I canna let you in herre. I wiel guv ham the watch forr you, if you like."

"No, I cannot do that," I replied. "This is a very expensive Rolex (which, if he had checked properly, he would have seen that it wasn't). I must give it to him personally".

"Sorry, sirr. Canna do that!"

"But if anything happens to this watch, we'll both be sacked!" I wailed.

That seemed to startle him and he wavered. But before he

could recover his composure, I exclaimed, "Oh, Look! There he is!"

Before the guy knew what was happening, I was past him. Once inside, I noticed an untended glass of beer on a table. I picked it up and went straight over to the window so that my friends could see me. There I was in the act of saluting the lads outside with my glass when I felt a hand on my shoulder. It belonged to Keith Mackenzie.

"What the hell are you doing in here?" he demanded. He then proceeded to march me back out through the locker rooms even more quickly than I had come in, although to the resounding cheers of my admiring colleagues.

My mission had been accomplished and it was the sweetest fiver I ever earned.

King of the Castle

I was born in Dublin, Ireland on September 17, 1939 to Jack and Julia O'Reilly. When I was growing up in the 1940s, Dublin Town was a fairly bleak place. But I have to say that while my brothers and sisters and I did not have any luxuries in our lives, we were never hungry or had to go to school unshod. My father was a Quartermaster Sergeant in the Irish Army and therefore knew the value of a pound and how to make it stretch. He had perfected the fine art of giving my mother the precise and exact amount of money she needed to feed and clothe us, no more and no less. He never left us short but neither was there ever anything left over for the nice things in life. From an early age my brothers, sisters, and I realised that if we wanted anything for ourselves we had to find a way to earn the wherewithal. Nobody was going to give us anything on a plate.

Due to his military training and background my father was a fairly hard bastard. When he said, "Jump" we did so—on the spot. He was used to giving orders and having them

*The O'Reilly family at Rathmines, Dublin in 1953. I am pictured here
with my sisters Veronica, Evelyn, and Sheila, and our father, Jack.*

obeyed. But, in fairness, most of the time he controlled us by
his loud bark rather than the force of his hand. In many
households in those bad old days, our contemporaries were
physically terrorised by their fathers. We did not suffer that.

My mother was always very gentle and kind and she sacri-
ficed everything for her childrens' well-being. Like many
women in those days she rarely left her home. She cooked
our meals and made sure we went to school on time and did
our homework properly. I liked school and was fairly good at
it. I remained there until the age of 16, which was two years
longer than most working-class kids back then. My first job
after leaving school was the fairly normal one of being a bicycle messenger boy. It did not last very long, however. On my
first day out on the bike I was supposed to deliver some
boxes of eggs, but the front wheel got caught up on some
streetcar lines that were all over the streets of Dublin at the
time. I fell off and my load of eggs shattered across the pave-
ment. It got me fired on the spot.

As I got a little older I discovered that I had a mechanical bent, so I took up an apprenticeship to become an aeroplane mechanic at Baldonnell Airport. Now, that would have been a lucrative and steady vocation if I had stuck with it. But I hated every minute of it. I found it boring to be scrambling around in a cold and greasy hangar tightening nuts and screws or whatever. Had they offered me a chance to learn how to fly the aeroplanes, now that would have been different! But they didn't, so I quit as soon as I could. Now please don't think that I am complaining about lost opportunities and riches. I have had a very exciting and interesting life, travelling all over the world, meeting many wonderful people and following the sun. Looking back, I think I instinctively realised that I would be happier living by my wits in the "service industry" rather than working on machines all day.

One day in the spring of 1947 (when I was eight years of age) my brothers, Michael, Noel, and I were in Rathmines village, close to where we lived. In the window of the local grocery shop we noticed an advertisement announcing that nearby Castle Golf Club was looking for young fellows to take up caddying duties. My oldest brother, Michael, said, "Lads, we should give that a try. That's money for old rope!"

So the three O'Reilly brothers presented themselves to the caddie master, Mr. George Webster, at the Castle Golf Club bright and early the very next morning, our minds racing with thoughts of the untold riches that we were about to get our greedy little paws on. Henceforth we would be able to buy our own sweets (candy) and comics as well as being able to go to the movies whenever we wished. Right from day one we gave Mother half of our earnings, whether it was six pence or a shilling. It seemed almost too good to be true to be paid for walking around in the fresh air for a couple of hours. Later on, we learned that if we could find a few lost golf balls in the high grass we could bring them home, fill up the cracks with putty and paint them with white shoe polish. Golf balls were so scarce in the 1940s that there was a brisk trade in used balls at every club in the country. We sold them back to the members without any fear of being reported for breaking the club rule against it. The shortage was so severe that everybody turned a blind eye to our enterprise because it was very important to keep enough golf balls in circulation, no matter how poor their condition. We did, however, receive the odd complaint from an irate member, someone who probably was unlucky enough to buy a particularly badly damaged ball that only took a shot or two to reveal its true state. But we only laughed because we knew there was nothing he could do about it. He had broken the rules, too, by buying the ball in the first place. As my caddying fee increased I was able to save a little and in due course bought a second-hand bicycle that I was very proud of.

Castle Golf Club had, and still has, a bit of a reputation for being one of Dublin's wealthiest, swankiest, and snobbiest clubs, with a lot of "old money" among the membership. This did not bother me in the slightest because it meant that I had a better chance of making a few extra bob. My father taught us to regard people as flesh and blood—no more and no less—just like ourselves, no matter who or what they were.

"They all have the same number of bones as you do," he would say with proud wisdom, "and they can only sleep in one bed."

As long as I was paid for my services, I did not care what place in society my employers might have belonged to, or what they thought of me. However, it did not take too long for me to learn that caddies should only be seen and not heard unless spoken to first, and that a polite, respectful silence increased the chances of repeat business and the size of my tip at the end of the day. Nobody likes an overly talkative, noisy, or shifty caddie.

When my father heard what his sons were up to, he called us together and told us very passionately that only those knighted by the King of England were entitled to be called "Sir." He seemed to have a bee in his bonnet about it.

"There are no 'Sirs' at the Castle," he said.

Perhaps he compared the golf club members to his own superior officers at the barracks and he did not want us giving them any more respect than was their due. There was to be no feelings of unnecessary inferiority. We asked him how we should address the golfers.

"Call them 'Mister.' This is a republic!" he thundered.

I did not have a clue what a republic was and when we got down to the club, Mr. Webster, of course, gave us completely contrary instructions. That put us in a dilemma. I decided to grasp the nettle and come clean with my very first client. I explained my predicament to Mr. Jim Egar. He was a kind and understanding fellow and he said he fully agreed with my father and I should indeed call him "Mister." I have never deviated from that practise since, no matter whose bag I have carried. Mr. Egar gave me a shilling and told me that I had been an excellent caddie for my first day and that I would soon be earning 1/6d. I was thrilled and ran all the way home to tell Mother.

I enjoyed being at the golf club. There were lots of other young lads like myself there and we were all great mates. While we waited for a bag (to be "jobbed," we called it), we made up our own golf matches, sharing clubs and balls to play on our own makeshift course behind the clubhouse. These were different times; there were no carts or trolleys and nobody would consider playing golf without a caddie back then. If you were prepared to stay at the club all day, you could usually get around three times—and more than that if only a nine-hole spin was involved. One day one of the people I often caddied for, a Mr. Naismith, gave me a hand-me-down 6-iron and the bug began to gnaw at me. From that moment on, if I was not out on the course caddying, I was behind the clubhouse increasing my shot-making ability with my proudest possession.

During the summer months the caddies were allowed play the course on Monday mornings. We soon began to organise competitions and they developed into fairly serious affairs. Some of the bigger boys were good players, especially the Kinsella boys, Jimmy and Billy, whose father, Bill, was the Castle Club professional. All of the Kinsellas were very tall and athletic and they could hit the ball out of sight. Par meant nothing to them. Jimmy was so strong that he had to have a second shaft inserted into the shaft in his driver to make it extra stiff (not unheard of in days gone by). He won the Irish Professional Championship twice (1972 and 1973) and also won the 1972 Madrid Open. Billy was a good player too. He went on to take up an appointment as head professional at Woodbrook Golf Club, south of Dublin, and served there for many years. Billy's son, David, has revived the connections with the Castle by returning there as head pro in recent years. Willie Holly, who I believe may have been one of the first players ever to use a 1- iron, also became a professional of some note. He never carried a wooden club in his bag, even when he competed for prize money. He told me that he had put a blowtorch to a 3-iron and had bent it to strengthen it. He could do mighty deeds with that homemade weapon. Willie was an excellent teacher and made his living at the Castle coaching the members all of his working life.

As I grew in confidence and began to feel very much at home I plucked up the courage to ask Mrs. Naismith if I could use her set of clubs in the caddie competitions because her husband's clubs were too heavy for me. The request was kindly granted and with a full artillery now at my disposal, I seemed to improve steadily week by week and my scores began to tumble. In due course I reached a four handicap and thought that I was "King of the Castle." I was invited to join the Irish Artisans' Society and allowed to play in their competitions at courses all over Dublin. The Artisans had some very good players in their ranks and those fellows knew the game of golf inside out. They taught me a lot. It was with the Artisans that I got my first inkling of perhaps trying to find a way to earn my future living through the game of golf.

One day, when I was only 12 years old, I was caddying for Mr. Naismith. He and his wife lived in a big house across the street from the golf club. Without a hint of warning Mr. Naismith suddenly keeled over on the second green and died. As he gasped for breath at my feet, I did not know what exactly was happening or what I should do next. His playing partners shouted at me to run to the clubhouse as quickly as possible and ask somebody to call a doctor and an ambulance. The club secretary told me to go across the street immediately and tell Mrs. Naismith "to come quick!" I ran like the wind to deliver my sad tidings. At that stage I was pushed into the background and took no further part in the day's tragic events. To tell you the truth, I went home feeling slightly bitter about the lengths to which some people would go to cheat you out of a lousy shilling. About six weeks later the secretary called me into his office. My suspicious nature led me to believe that I was in for the "high jump" (about to be punished) for some forgotten past transgression. To my surprise, though, he handed me a brown envelope.

"Mrs. Naismith asked me to give you this," the secretary said, "and to thank you for your efforts when her husband passed away."

When I opened the envelope and found a five-pound note inside, I was flabbergasted. This was enormous, inconceivable money to me. When I handed it up to my mother she was very suspicious and it took a little bit of persuasion on my part to reassure her that the fortune had not been ill-gotten. She would never have tolerated that.

On another occasion, I did find myself in hot water and on the wrong side of the law. Going down Crannagh Road on our way home from the golf club one evening with my brother Noel, the hunger pangs overcame us and we hopped over a low wall and helped ourselves to some of the most gorgeous apples and pears you ever saw. It turned out that the reason they were so nice was because they were prize exhibits being lovingly cultivated for the upcoming Dublin

Horticultural Show. The owner, a Mr. Hunt (I will never forget him), almost frothed at the mouth when he caught us red-handed. I thought he was going to kill us right there on the spot. Instead, he called the guards (police) and pressed charges. We were brought to court the next morning and had to appear before Judge Farrell who was one of my "regulars" at the Castle. He seemed very stern in the precincts of his court. He gave us a severe tongue-lashing and fined each of us two shillings which was an awful lot of money. It would take us a while to save that up. Just before he dismissed us, however, Judge Farrell discreetly got my attention. "Reilly, will I see you at the Castle on Thursday?" he whispered.

"Yes, Your Honour," says I.

"Good. Be on the first tee at 1 o'clock."

I was very nervous going to the golf club that Thursday but a promise is a promise and I never missed an appointment on purpose in my life. Still, I was trembling at what the judge might say and do. Would he bring me before the Secretary and have me sacked? Were my caddying days at the Castle over? My father had told me to go down there "like a man and face the music." When we had completed the round (during which my misdemeanour was never once mentioned), Judge Farrell said, "Reilly, your debt to society has been paid."

It was the one and only time that I was actually relieved *not* to receive my caddie fee. The good Judge had personally paid the fine on my behalf and that was the end of that. I was delighted and most grateful. I gave his clubs and shoes an extra bit of elbow grease that afternoon. And Noel and I never looked at an apple again, no matter how hungry we were.

My eldest brother, Michael, eventually drifted away from caddying, leaving Noel and myself a free run at it. Like our father, Michael was a steadying influence and a stickler for probity, whereas Noel and I were both a pair of rascals. There was a tradition at the Castle that if a player scored a hole-in-one, his caddie would receive a 2/6d. bonus (half a dollar). Noel and I, therefore, concocted a scheme that if one of us was loose while the other was "jobbed" (caddying), the free one would lurk in the trees behind the thirteenth green. While the players were walking toward the green and out of sight down in the deep dip in front, the ball nearest the hole would be deposited by hand into the cup. The ensuing half crown spoils would be divided later. Mr. Jim Egar was our first victim. He had poor eyesight and we got away with it. A few weeks later we successfully repeated the scam. Egar was the talk of the club, with his two holes in one at the same hole within a month. But much against my wishes, Noel became greedy and went for the hat trick. Unfortunately, he got caught. Because I was on Egar's bag, I had an alibi and got off scot-free. Noel was suspended from caddying for a year. He was bigger than I was and he walloped me all the way home, saying it was all my fault—that I should have delayed the players when they were down in the dip. I replied, "It is you who got caught, not me."

Avoiding getting caught has been a kind of a life principle with me ever since that day. The greatest crime of all, though, is to be caught in the act. I do not think Noel ever forgave me.

When I had graduated to the status of number one caddie, I was entitled to go out with the biggest tipper in the club, Mr. P.J. Carroll of the Tobacco Empire. In spite of being a lousy golfer, he paid me a highly desirable half-crown for my services. He always smoked his own very special cigarettes, which he kept in a fancy silver case in his golf bag. At the Castle, the golfers had a long walk back to the fifth tee box after they had completed the fourth hole. I always handed my player the driver and walked forward to ball spot (fore caddie). Since the fairway was blind from the tee, I would then help myself to one of those special cigarettes, thus getting hooked on a habit that I have never been able to break to this day. I lit up for a few quick drags before I put the fag out and stuck it in my pocket for more leisurely use later. This went on for some time until one day Mr. Carroll shocked me by paying me only one shilling and sixpence instead of the usual amount.

"Reilly," he explained, "I am deducting you a shilling in lieu of all the cigarettes that you have removed from my golf bag without my permission."

"But, but, but, Mr. Carroll ..."

"But nothing, Reilly. I have been watching you send smoke signals from behind the rise on the fifth fairway for months."

It was a fair cop; I hadn't a leg to stand on. The next time we went out together, Mr. Carroll offered me a cigarette as we left the fourth green and all seemed to be forgiven. (It should have been because I became Carroll's biggest customer!)

Another famous Castle member was Spencer Freeman, the founder and Boss of the Irish Hospital Sweepstakes. Back in the 1950s, the Sweep was equivalent to the National Lottery except that it was a worldwide phenomenon. This guy was mega rich. He had a chauffeur who drove him around in an enormous Lincoln automobile, possibly the only one in the whole country. Like the professional golfers of today, Mr. Freeman arrived dressed for action. He always wore plus fours and changed his shoes on the running board. He was a resonable golfer who always played solo and was a bit of a fitness fanatic. After completing nine holes he would take off his jacket, hand it to me, tell me to take it and his clubs back to the chauffeur and wait for him. Then he would set off to briskly jog the back nine with a peculiar high stepping action. Occasionally, but not very often, he would take one club with him and hit a shot or two on his way. When he had finished his run, he would pay me two shillings and offer me a lift home. Boy, did I enjoy that ride! It was like being a "rich kid." Freeman allowed me to sit in front with the driver while he sat in the rear. He seemed to get a great kick out of seeing my pals rushing up to look inside the Lincoln when we arrived at Rathmines Town Hall where I was always let off. He was a kind man and often gave the other children a few pennies for sweets. I suspect that it may have been his purpose all along.

One Tuesday afternoon I did not get a bag and I wandered off down by the stream at the seventh hole, looking for golf balls. I came upon a nest with two fine big duck eggs sitting in it. I remembered my mother saying that duck eggs were good for you.

"They taste strong but they're very good for you," she said.

I took them and put one in each pocket of my jacket. I did not realise that I was being watched by one of the workmen on the course. He told the new caddie master, Pat White. When I came back up from my wandering, White caught me and clapped his hands against my two hip pockets, smashing the eggs and making an awful mess inside.

"That'll teach you to go stealing duck eggs," he sneered.

My mother was not too pleased, either, especially when she saw the mess that my jacket was in when I got home.

There was also Mr. Des Stevens, a member who played every Wednesday. He was the owner of a bicycle shop at the top of Grafton Street and was guilty of the crime of being the first businessman to import the dreaded trolley (pull cart) into Ireland. Since he was responsible for so much unemployment among caddies, I should have organised it that every caddie in Ireland would have had the pleasure of letting air out of his tyres.

Another famous person for whom I caddied at the Castle was David Love. He was a very wealthy property owner all over Dublin. He also bred the horse Larkspur that won the Derby. Then there was Tommy Loader and Gordon Greene. If you caddied for any of those gentlemen you were paid top dollar.

Every Monday I caddied for a Mr. Ward. He owned two movie theatres in Rathmines, the "Princess" and the "Stella." The former was for the riffraff and the latter was for the more well-off. Every time I caddied for Ward he gave me two tickets for the Sunday afternoon show at the Stella. I used to sell these more expensive tickets so that my sisters and brothers and I could all go to the Princess with the proceeds. One Monday Mr. Ward called me aside and asked how I had enjoyed the movie the previous afternoon. I told him that it was great. But then he asked me what was the name of the movie and what was it about. Of course, I did not have a clue. That put a stop to my free tickets and my sisters were rightly fed up with me.

Finally, there was Bobby McTear who owned T.E.K. Dairies in Ranelagh, not far from my home. He left instructions that whenever I called to his depot I should be given as much milk, buttermilk, and cream as I could carry home. My mother was always delighted with this little bonus, especially the buttermilk, which she used for baking cakes.

All in all, the members at the Castle were very good to me. They taught me a lot about golf and life; I learned the value of a good work ethic. I found out that if I took good care of my clients, they would look after me, too. It was perfect training for when I became a professional caddie because the same rules applied. Therefore, I learned early in life that it paid to be reliable. So, I pitched up at the Castle no matter if there was hail, rain, or snow because if there was no golf, I usually was paid anyway.

"No golf today, Reilly," one of the members would say. "But thanks for coming up just in case. Here's sixpence." If more than three of the golfers gave me a tanner (sixpence) it was as good a return as if I had been out caddying. No wonder my mother said to me, "Johnny, you'll never be short of a few shillings. You have always had the knack of earning it. You will get on well in this world."

How right she was.

The Players

I caddied for so many players over the years that it is impossible to remember them, let alone try to mention them all here. During my professional career, I had three main employers: Peter Townsend (seven years); Des Smyth (15 years); and Padraig Harrington (three years). Townsend won three European Tour events. He also earned Ryder Cup, Walker Cup, and World Cup "caps." He won in 12 countries around the globe and is a past Captain of the British PGA. These days he is a consultant on golf course design issues with the European Tour and still competes from time to time on the European Seniors Tour.

Des Smyth is one of the longest surviving players on the European Tour, having earned his card for the first time in 1974. The winner of eight European titles over three decades, he has played on two Ryder Cup teams, won the Irish National Championship five times, and was victorious in numerous other regional and unofficial events. He was a member of the Irish team that won the Dunhill Cup in 1988 and, in 2001, became the oldest player ever to win on the European Tour when he won the Madeira Open at age 47.

Padraig Harrington was a three-time member of the Walker Cup team before he turned professional in 1996. Since then (as of this writing), he has won four times on the European Tour, finished second 17 times, and is among the world's top 10 players according to the Sony rankings. He was one of only 19 players who made the cut in all four of golf's major championships in 2000, including an honourable, if distant (to Tiger Woods) fifth in the U.S. Open at Pebble Beach. Padraig made an excellent Ryder Cup debut at The Country Club in Brookline, Massachusetts in 1999.

Pete "Tiddler" Townsend (1975 to 1982)

Peter Townsend was my first regular bag on the professional golf tour. I had caddied for him off and on at Portmarnock (where he was the head professional) and elsewhere around Ireland before he invited me to go with him full-time on the European tour after we had "done" a successful Irish Open together. I accepted with enthusiasm because the spirit of adventure attracted me. Besides, I was in trouble with my employers at C.I.E. (the local transport company) for whom I had graduated from Bus Conductor to full Driver status. Much as I liked driving, the long, rigid working hours (especially the night shift) were depressing. I could not get the fresh air, freedom, and excitement of caddying out of my system. So whenever there was a big tournament in Dublin, I phoned in sick and pursued my love of caddying. Somebody in the Personnel Department must have noticed the pattern, however, because I was caught on camera while caddying for Peter in the Irish Open at Portmarnock when I should have been at the wheel of the 78A. But before the company could take any action against me, I quit and took up Townsend's glamorous-sounding offer.

I remained on tour with Peter for seven happy and eventful

years. Unwittingly, he trained me well. He was a Dr. Jekyll and Mr. Hyde character, which meant life was not dull anymore and he helped me to become an amateur golf psychologist as a sideline. A charming and highly intelligent person off the golf course, Peter's moods were unpredictable on it and I had to learn how to cope. Overall he treated me very well and I have no complaints. He was my meal ticket for seven years. I was prepared to put up with a lot for that and the privilege of learning my trade. Sometimes I half expected to see him growing horns and a tail on the course. Boy, did he make me sweat when that happened! But I also got used to it and learned how to work around it by keeping my mouth shut and staying as quiet and as docile as a church mouse.

Peter was a tremendous player, but he grew more and more frustrated as the seasons went by because he never reached his full potential in professional golf. He should have been a world-beater, a top-20-world-rankings-kind-of-guy, if there had been such a thing back then. His underachieving was clearly caused by tentative putting. From tee to green he was as good as the best, but on the green he was a "nervous Nellie." He continually allowed tension to creep in and suffocate him. When he began freezing over his putts, I used to nearly cry just watching him. I did my best to try and get him to relax but those little horns would start to appear and I would beat a hasty retreat. Still he managed to win in some very exotic locations, 12 countries in all. But his record in Europe bore no resemblance or justice to his talents. It was a shame because everyone thought that Peter Townsend had at least one British Open victory in him—he was that good. I stayed with him until 1982, when he finally gave up tormenting himself. I think he was pretty disillusioned about the game by the end of his career. He was fortunate, though, because he started a new career as a big wheel in the PGA and then as a consultant with the golf course development wing of the European Tour.

The last time I caddied for Peter was a highly memorable

occasion, although I'm sure he would not like to be reminded of it. He was playing in the Irish Professional Match-Play championship at Rosslare and was having a great battle with Paddy Skerritt, that most genial of players from Lahinch and St. Anne's. We were the last group on the course and after 18 holes, the match was all-square. Sudden death was needed to decide who would go on to the next round. At the nineteenth, Peter played an excellent approach shot into the middle of the green. Paddy came up short with his and was about 50 feet from the putting surface. When we walked onto the green, Peter noticed that the hole position had been prematurely changed for the following day's play and he was not quite as close as he should have been. Naturally, he created a bit of a fuss and demanded that the hole be recut in its original position. He was quite within his rights, of course, so the Tournament Director had no choice but to comply. Rules are rules. But ... where was the greenskeeper? It turned out that the fellow had been at the course since 5 a.m. and had already gone home. After a delay of nearly an hour and with darkness falling rapidly, he was finally discovered in a local hostelry, uprooted and forced to return to change the hole back to where it had been in the first place. The story then took the inevitable golfing twist. Paddy Skerritt, who had nonchalantly smiled his way through the entire hubbub, holed his putt from over 15 yards! Peter, of course, missed his. To this day, I am certain that if he had not said anything and accepted the situation as it was presented to him in the first place, he would have won the match. But that's golf. And sometimes it pays not to be too picky and just get on with things.

It often seems as if only a player's wife and his caddie really know what makes a guy tick. Peter had the most beautiful wife. Lorna was an absolute treasure. We often compared notes to test the "mood temperature," and then did our best to put Peter in the right frame of mind. Whenever he flew off the handle at me, Lorna used to say, "Don't take it from him, Johnny. Tell him to carry his own bloody bag!"

I was only one of millions who were in love with Lorna because she frequently appeared in commercials on TV and was a famous fashion model in London and Dublin. Sadly, she died young and it was a dreadful shock when it happened. Lorna and the late Vivienne Jacklin were great pals on the Tour whenever they decided to follow the sun and their men. I was occasionally given the job of acting as their minder and driver. One of my fondest memories is of bringing the pair of them down to the seaside village of Howth during the Irish Open at Portmarnock, where they enjoyed some "girl talk" and a few half-pints of Guinness (no self-respecting lady would be seen drinking a pint). It is hard to believe that neither of those gorgeous, warm-hearted, and amusing ladies is with us any longer. Both died prematurely and have gone to the great clubhouse in the sky.

Peter and Lorna went on a nongolfing trip once and they asked me to keep an eye on their magnificent house at Howth, which is one of the most beautiful spots in Ireland. It is an old working seaside village north of Dublin with some lovely old houses, pubs, walks, and views. Naturally, I was flattered to be asked. Unfortunately, I also let temptation get the better of me. Every once in a while, on our way home from a tournament, Peter would allow me to drive his gorgeous Jaguar XJ-12 motorcar while he took a nap. Well, there she was, sitting all alone in the garage. In all fairness, I felt the car could do with a short spin up to the summit of Howth hill to catch some of the brilliant fresh air to be had up there. There was also a nice hotel with a lovely bar on the summit, and it featured a magnificent view of the Irish Sea and Dublin Bay. The Jaguar would like that, I thought.

Anyhow, in the pub, I got to chatting with two nice ladies. When they asked me if I might give them a lift to Sutton, not far away, I was only too pleased to oblige and show off "my" vehicle. Everything went smooth as silk until I got back to the pub. My parking space had been taken while I was away and there was none to be had anywhere. I was very much in need of a nightcap so I drove around the back and parked the Jag next to a big, dirty skip. My nightcap turned into two or three and when I came out to go home I could not find that beautiful XJ-12 to save my life! After a frantic half-hour of searching, I walked to the police station and reported the car as stolen. The "boys in blue" were most helpful. They put me in a squad car and drove me all over Howth looking for Peter's car. Eventually, somebody came up with the bright idea that we should take a look behind the hotel. To my great relief, there was "Melissa" in all her glory. The policemen, not surprisingly, were not amused. They gave me a good bollocking and told me that if they ever saw me driving Townsend's car again they would report that fact to him.

I never again took that chance and liberty.

Des Smyth (1982 to 1996)

In 1982 at Troon, Des Smyth came within a whisker of winning the 111th Open Championship. He was tied for the lead on the fifteenth tee in the final round but Tom Watson put in a stronger finish and that was that. The two-shot margin may as well have been 20, as far as taking home the ancient claret jug was concerned. Although I had worked for him occasionally, I had not taken up with "Smythie" on a regular basis by the time of the '82 Open. I have often wondered how it would have felt to have been in the "eye" of a major championship like the Open, all the way down to the wire. How would I have coped? Could I have made a difference? Interesting questions that will never be answered.

Smythie's caddie at Troon was a venerable Englishman known as "Squeaky" who had had enough of hardship and travel and wanted to retire. Des decided he would be better off with a fellow countryman on his bag, and since he knew that Townsend was thinking of leaving the scene, too, he approached me at Fulford a few weeks after the Open. I was interested, all right, but I could not dump Peter after being

Des Smyth and I inspect the "ammo" before entering battle.

with him for seven years. I told Des that as soon as
Townsend quit the tournament scene for good at the end of
the season, I would then go with him. Smythie was
impressed. "Fair dues, O'Reilly. I admire your loyalty."

Loyalty has always been important to me. It is one of my
proudest boasts that in all my years of caddying, I have never
missed a tee-time and never been sacked. Put in the dog-
house? Yes. Reprimanded? Yes. Rested? Yes. But an outright
sacking? Never.

I was not with Smythie for very long before I decided that I
had to review my damaging lifestyle. We were playing in the
British PGA Championship at Sandwich in the south of England
and were paired with "the merry Mex," Lee Trevino. I had had
a particularly bad "night before" and was very hungover.

When Smythie asked me for the golf balls so that he could mark them, Trevino noticed my hand shake.

"Is Johnny nervous?" he asked Smythie teasingly.

"I doubt it," said Des, laughing. But he was not laughing about an hour later on the blind fifth hole when I gave him a hopeless yardage because I checked it off the wrong sprinkler head, causing him to come up short by 30 yards after hitting a beauty.

"Give me that book and I want to see you in my office after the round!" were the last words he spoke to me for three tense and anxious hours. The "office," of course, was Des's car in the car park. I knew immediately that I was in big trouble. Bad news travels fast; all of the other caddies were agog with the rumour that "Reilly is for the high jump!"

"It is like this, Johnny," Des said to me later, "you can either give up the drink or give up caddying for me."

I made the right choice and did not touch a drop of alcohol of any kind for two years after that. Thankfully I never recovered the drinking habit to the extent that I once had it. Staying away from booze made a big difference, not only in the way that I was perceived but in the way that I perceived myself. The Smyth/Reilly combination went from strength to strength and I was treated to front-row viewing of hundreds of outstanding golfing moments subsequently.

If I had £1 for every time that I have been asked to describe the best shot I ever saw, I would be very rich indeed. I think it may have been the one I saw Smythie play at Connemara during the Irish Match-Play championship in 1980, which strangely enough was before I became his regular Tour caddie. I am sure that Ciaran Monaghan, who is Head Pro at Druid's Glen these days, and Smythie's opponent on that memorable day, has not forgotten the shot, either.

On the crest of his overseas successes, playing in a domestic event was regarded as a week off—holiday golf, more or less. Smythie, however, was still expected to perform well and win. We faced Monaghan in the quarterfinal match.

After a sluggish front nine, Des began to chip away at his opponent's lead. But it was looking grim when he was still one down playing No. 18, and it got even worse when his approach overshot the green and settled into a horrible place. Meanwhile, Ciaran played onto the front edge but a long way from the hole.

Now, the green at 18 sloped severely from back to front and there were several "elephants" buried in it to complicate matters further. Adding to the problem was the fact that Des was in high grass, halfway up what I can only describe as a steep wall of ground. It was clearly a shot for Spiderman. Smythie marched up and down surveying the scene while I looked on wondering how I would get back to Dublin that evening because there was no way he was going to get himself out of this mess. I could clearly hear the spectators muttering "No chance" in the background and I was definitely inclined to agree with them.

Finally, Des says, "Reilly, give me the Unique."

I must say that I have never seen another professional golfer carry a club quite like this one. Unique it certainly was. It had a face as big as a shovel, the angle where the head joined the hosel was set slightly forward to eliminate any possibility of a dreaded shank, and it had an extraordinary wide, flanged, and concave sole. After taking great care to build his stance (within the rules) he took a full, wide swing. Grass flew everywhere and the ball came out as slowly as a butterfly. It floated through the air, almost in slow motion, landed as soft as you like on the sloping green, and drifted down next to the cup. The crowd stood there stunned, and Monaghan looked as if he had received an electric shock. He three-putted tamely, then capitulated without a fight on the first extra hole—that's how shattered he was. With that near miss behind him, Smythie's game face came on. A win is a win ... anytime, anywhere. And when things got tight at the finishing line, professional pride and the killer instinct became factors in the equation. Des went into top gear the next day and gave David Jones from Bangor a five and four drubbing in the final. Over the years, Des Smyth's short game has always been phenomenal. It's what has kept him competitive for 27 years, as long as anybody on tour. That shot at Connemara was no fluke.

Another of my favourite moments of all the time with Des was when we went to Ronan Rafferty's club, Warrenpoint in Northern Ireland, for a charity event. It was one of the first times that I can remember a bookmaker being allowed onto a golf course. This was an overdue development because it created an extra bit of interest for the spectators, players, and caddies alike. It was a good facility to have because we could go into the marquee to study the form, place a few bets on the golf or the horses, and then watch the action on television if we felt like it. The amount of time spent hanging around waiting on the golf circuit is probably its biggest drawback. Any diversion is good, in my opinion. Allowing the bookies in certainly helped to break the monotony for me.

Although Smythie was cock-of-the-walk among the Irish players on the European Tour at the time, and playing in one-day domestic events was only a doddle to him, the Warrenpoint bookie did not seem to know it. Which was probably why he quoted Des at the unbelievable odds of 16/1. Naturally, Smythie and I had to have a piece of that action. Then, after the tournament produced a tie between Denis Durnian, Roger Chapman, and Smythie, the misguided bookie announced new prices on the outcome of the impending play-off: Durnian 4/6; Chapman evens; Smythie 7/4. Unbelievable! We dived in again and had another "cut."

Believe me, we really cleaned that golf-ignorant bookie out, lock, stock, and barrel. Going home later that evening the floor of Smythie's car was strewn with money in all denominations. Cheques, dollars, sterling, punts—you name it, we had it. At the border between Northern Ireland and the Republic, we were stopped by a patrol. One of the soldiers looked into the car and saw money all over the place.

"Where did yiz get all that money?" he asked.

"We robbed it off a stupid North of Ireland bookie!" I told him.

Smythie roared with laughter then explained our little coup. Fortunately the soldier had heard of Des and recognised him. He said he was delighted for us. "It is always great to see one being put over the bookies!" he called after us.

Like many other Irish pros (for some inexplicable reason), Smythie was very lucky in Spain. He won the lucrative Sanyo tournament and the Madrid Open as well. We always seemed to make a good amount of pesetas. When he won the Sanyo at El Prat in Barcelona, it was quite extraordinary. On day one (Thursday) we set off in what we would describe in Ireland as "a sight of rain." After nine holes, Smythie was seven over par and clearly had no chance of making the cut. On the tenth tee, he wistfully watched the planes taking off from the airport that is located right beside the golf course and then made the following never-to-be-forgotten comment:

"Reilly, we'll be on one of those planes and out of here this evening."

We were playing with Ronan Rafferty who was four under at the same stage and leading the tournament. Suddenly, the siren went off and we were all called in off the golf course, which was then declared unplayable. To everybody's amazement, the day's scores were all scrubbed. Those going badly received a "full pardon" and those who had scored well, doubtless felt aggrieved. It did not matter if anybody thought it was unfair—that is the way the cookie crumbles. We started with a clean sheet on Friday and struggled around in 72. On Saturday, Des shot lights out for a 66. It was the best round of the day and he won a fabulous state-of-the-art music centre from the sponsors in the process.

"That made all the hanging around worthwhile," he said.

Des stayed near the lead throughout Sunday until he came to the seventeenth hole, which was a semiblind, uphill par 3 of about 175 yards. After long deliberation, we chose a 6-iron.

Because of the awful weather, the only spectator was a lone Spanish soldier standing motionless behind the green. I have no idea why he was there.

"Hit it at your man behind the green," says I. Des hit a beauty. "That is close!" exclaimed our South African playing companions, John Bland and Hugh Baiocchi, almost in unison. When we got to the green, however, there were only two balls visible. I was puzzled. The soldier had not moved a muscle. He must have known nothing about golf because as I walked past the cup I glanced into the hole — more out of habit than hope — and there she was. A hole-in-one.

"I think there's a car for the first hole-in-one during the tournament," Baiocchi said to Des.

Smythie was almost jumping up and down with excitement. We were unsure if the prize applied to the seventeenth hole or not, but he was in no mood to wait to find out. He ordered me to immediately head for the clubhouse to clarify matters.

"Give me my driver and go find out if I've won the car!"

Reaching the Tournament Director's office in the clubhouse, I breathlessly reported our good fortune. The man I spoke to was a Spaniard who spoke with a Dublin accent that was even thicker than mine was, but he definitely confirmed that there was a beautiful Volvo for the first ace on *any* hole, and it was ours! Back down to the eighteenth green I scrambled. As soon as I was within sight of Smythie, I gave him the thumbs up. He did a little hop, shrieked with delight, completely lost his concentration and carelessly three putted. But it didn't matter because the gods were completely on our side that week. Fortunately, he would have time to recover his composure overnight because it was decided to extend play into Monday. A very rare event.

I, on the other hand, had a most uncomfortable Sunday night. My body was used to a bit of relaxation after a hard week. I never work on Mondays and I was bemoaning our luck that the tournament had not been reduced to 54 holes. Smythie, however, played beautifully on the final day and climaxed the round with a birdie on the last hole. He just squeezed past Sam Torrance and won the whole ball of wax. Unbelievably, from a hopeless position after his initial nine holes, Des had managed to come back and win a fantastic music centre, a fabulous car, and a big tournament all in one fell swoop. If I were Ronan Rafferty, I would have to wonder about the power of fate.

Apart from winning the World Cup with Harrington and Paul McGinley at Kiawah, the next biggest win that I was involved in was undoubtedly the Dunhill Cup at St. Andrews in 1988. It was so exciting and full of incident. Ronan Rafferty, Eamon Darcy, and Smythie represented Ireland and fought their way into the semifinal stage to face England. Smythie was drawn to play Nick Faldo and it turned out to be a tense battle all the way. Smythie had the putter working nicely and was one up coming down the stretch. It was a typical October day in Scotland: dark, drizzly, and overcast. A mist off the sea made visibility troublesome. After a half at seventeen, we went to Tom Morris, the home hole at St. Andrews, one up and with the team result depending on our match.

Faldo was complaining that he could not see properly. Under those conditions, it was a fair comment. Smythie, however, was anxious to bring matters to a conclusion. He said to Faldo, "Let's get on with it and finish, if at all possible."

They both hit good drives over the road when the mist seemed to get even colder and thicker. Smythie still wanted to finish. It was his turn to play, so he went ahead and hit his approach shot into the mist toward a flag that was barely visible. Unfortunately, he overhit the target by 30 feet. Not a disaster, but not good, either. Faldo, still complaining about the lack of visibility, refused to budge and would not play his pitch. The spectators, the press, and the organisers were all extremely annoyed with him, but Nick dug in his heels. If golf were a popularity contest, nobody would have ever heard of Faldo. But that stubborn streak of his was the main reason why he was so successful. Far better to be at the top of the order of merit than at the top of a popularity contest. He certainly was an unpopular Nick Faldo that evening and was roasted unmercifully by the tabloids the following morning. But the man was quite within his rights.

At the crack of dawn the next morning, with a cold, sharp wind cutting through us, we gathered to finish the match. Des was on the practise green working on a putt similar to the one he was about to face, while Faldo was rehearsing his 80-yard pitch shots. Fanny Sunesson, Faldo's caddie, and I shivered as we looked on. Overnight Faldo had somehow become a hate figure because of the way the Scottish media targeted him. That he was English probably did not help either. Half of Scotland seemed to have turned up to cheer on their Celtic brothers, the Irish. The total student population of St. Andrews University, which overlooks the eighteenth green, was hanging out of their windows waving derogatory placards — about Faldo in particular and the English race in general. It was unreal and over the top, but it was in our favour.

In as hostile an environment as I can ever remember Faldo hit a nearly perfect shot to within about nine feet right of the cup. Smythie's poor effort was four feet short, leaving him with the worst putt on the Old Course at St. Andrews. Tantalisingly, Faldo's ball seemed to be willed out of the hole by the combined wishes of the biased onlookers. Dear Old Des then stood up to the pressure and banged his putt straight in. Delirium followed, but it was short-lived. We had to go out more or less immediately and try to do it all over again in the finals against the top-seeded Australians.

In the afternoon, things were not looking good as we reached the tee at the Road Hole (No. 17), one of the most famous shots in golf. The news had filtered back that once again it all depended on Smythie — and we were one down! Australia's Rodger Davis was playing steadily and solidly with no signs of weakness, so it was clear that Smythie would have to produce something special to overtake him. Rodger, however, played all of his shots with a big cut. Unfortunately for him, the correct tee shot at the Road Hole was not his favourite cup of tea. As we stood there in the tension of the moment, that portion of the Old Course Hotel ahead of us loomed larger than usual.

Every time an event was being filmed at St. Andrews by Sky Sports, my TV producer pal, Pat Furlong, would stand at the corner of the dogleg and direct television matters. I often chatted with him as we passed by, or if we happened to bump into each other in a pub downtown afterward. This day, as we waited for Davis to hit his tee shot, I could see Furlong in his usual spot. Almost immediately after Rodger let it fly, my buddy gave me a thumbs-down sign. I turned to Smythie. "That ball is in Room 110. It is out!"

"What do you mean?" says Rodger. "It can't be."

"How do you know?" asked Smythie. The veracity of the information was vital to whatever decision he might make about his tactical approach to the playing of the hole.

"The Sky TV guy down at the corner signalled me," I replied.

Rodger nearly collapsed into a heap on the tee. Smythie steered his drive around the corner but he left himself a long way back, the dangerous Road Bunker directly on his line in to the flag. Rodger became even more upset at this point and he hit another bad tee shot. It meant that he had little chance of doing better than a seven. After due deliberation, Smythie announced to me what he was going to do. It turned out to be one of the cleverest shots I have ever seen played. He purposely aimed well beyond the green onto the eighteenth tee, which took all of the trouble out of play. From there, it was a fairly easy chip and he duly made his par for a three-shot swing. We were now two shots in front with one hole to go. In desperation, Davis birdied the last but there was no way that lead would be given up. Smythie made a three as well and little Ireland had won the Dunhill Cup. The victory was even more enjoyable because it was such a huge upset.

Mark "Jesse" James

"What are you laughing at, Reilly?" Mark James asked.

"You," says I.

"Well, if I were you," he said, "I would be laughing at me, too."

"Jesse" had just hit four balls "out of town" from the twelfth tee at the Benson and Hedges Open at Fulford, one of the most important events on the European Tour calendar once upon a time. After the first one—without changing his normally doleful expression or even looking up from the ground—the former Ryder Cup captain merely stretched out his hand in the general direction of his caddie, John Moorehouse. "Ball, please."

Then another and another and another. After the fourth one, I could not contain myself any longer and I began to laugh. Mark, however, was well beyond being put off or miffed by my disrespect. In a matter-of-fact tone, he said, "I am going to stay here until I hit a (bleeping) ball in this (bleeping) fairway."

When the fifth effort was successful, Mark promptly turned on his heels with a curt "Cheerio, I am off" and walked back to the clubhouse to retire from the tournament. "Hurt" was the reason given later. Well, I can assure you that the only hurt incurred was to his ego. But it was also a wise move because otherwise he would have been up before the stewards and forced to pay a heavy fine.

Once upon a time, Mark James was the "enfant terrible" of the European Tour and regularly in hot water. In truth, though, there was no real harm in him, and in spite of the image that was often presented on TV, he was entertaining to be around. He was certainly a lot different than the average pro golfer, many of whom can be humourless, colourless, and downright boring.

I always admired Jesse's quirky self-deprecating and completely honest approach to golf. No whinging excuses came from him if things did not go his way. He never blamed his caddie when a wrong clubbing decision was made, unlike some others that I could mention.

"I take full responsibility for all decisions," he tells his caddies.

Playing in Sardinia some years ago, there was an acute shortage of caddies. The place was too inaccessible and expensive to get to for the less-dedicated and less-affluent bagmen and the locals knew absolutely nothing about golf. Therefore, most of the players decided to pull their own bags on trolleys. After a dreadful opening nine holes, Mark proceeded to play the second nine one-handed, pulling the trolley and swinging at the ball at the same time. Naturally, this unusual technique caused his score to rocket into the nineties with some ease. I heard that he was fined rather heavily for that minor display of petulance.

Personally, I have always enjoyed being in Mark's company. His morose demeanour and mournful expression on the golf course are deceptive. He's a very funny guy and his brand of humour has helped him to stand apart. He can play a gritty, admirable game when in the right mood, too.

Bernhard "The Red Baron" Langer

Bernie "The Red Baron" Langer is without a doubt the most conscientious and hard-working player I have ever seen. Vijay Singh and Harrington are the only serious rivals to the man's dedication and work ethic. The man is iron-willed, and he sticks to his game plan better than anyone. The way he managed to overcome the most severe and debilitating doses of the "yips" on three separate occasions is the most courageous and heart-warming effort that I have seen from any professional golfer. I have had the opportunity to study Bernhard's game up close many times and he controls the distance he hits the ball with every club better than anyone in the world of professional golf. "Being able to hit a golf ball the correct distance every time is even more valuable than being able to hit straight," he will tell you.

My admiration for Bernhard became personal and eternal when he was paired with Harrington in the Italian Open. Padraig and I had a lengthy discussion about a shot. It was one of those "Should I or shouldn't I go for it?" deals at an unreachable par 5. With my full encouragement, Padraig went flat out for it. Unfortunately though, the result was exactly what we were trying to avoid; the ball finished up in a cross bunker in front of the green 260 yards away. Harrington grumbled and tried to blame me but Bernhard jumped to my defence. "Don't blame Johnny," he told Padraig. "You could hit another 10 shots from there without reaching that trap. It was just one of those things."

There was no reason for Langer to say a word; it really was none of his business. But because of the respect that Padraig has for Bernhard, Harrington shut up straight away and never said another word about it.

Slammin' Sam Snead

By far, the most difficult person I ever had the "pleasure" of caddying for was "Slammin' Sammy" Snead because he was such a cranky perfectionist and so demanding. Sam worked me to the bone and had me under so much pressure I nearly ended up with a nervous breakdown by the end of the week. Sam left everybody with absolutely no doubt that he considered himself to be "camping out" because he was in Ireland playing in the Kerrygold Classic at Waterville. Snead had been enticed into coming to Kerry by a hefty appearance fee and the thought of a unique first prize: a bar of gold shaped like a pound of butter. It turned out that Tony Jacklin won the "butter," thanks to an unorthodox last day draw that allowed him to go out first in the final round even though he was leading the tournament. Apparently, he had to catch a flight to the United States. That rather unfair concession was crucial because it gave him the best of the weather conditions. The day deteriorated sharply for the late starters and their chances were blown away by the wind and rain.

The weather was typically Irish all week : sun, wind, rain—even hailstones. Sam found it highly perplexing and kept telling me so.

At the short par-3 seventh, which was played over water *and* into the wind, Sam asked me what stick did I think it was.

"It is a good 5 iron," says I, sagely.

"The being good does not arise!" replied Sam haughtily, basically meaning that *all* of his shots were "good." I suppose that kind of arrogance was the secret of why he was so successful.

What Sam did that week when he was away from the golf course remains a mystery. After each round, while he was checking his scorecard, he sent me into the locker room for his street shoes. Like Spencer Freeman at the Castle, he changed from his golf shoes beside the eighteenth green and handed them to me to be put into his locker overnight. He then stepped into an enormous opaque-windowed chauffeur-driven limousine and sped off. Nobody ever saw a car like it in County Kerry before. Nor did anyone get to see who or what else was inside the huge automobile. Prompted by the press guys, I did my best to find out. But try as I might, I failed. Several times I asked Sam for a lift back to town but I was denied every time. Where he went, where he stayed, and most important with whom, is still the talk of the town of Waterville 30 years later.

"Irish" Bob Murphy

On another occasion at the Waterville-Kerrygold Classic, I caddied for "Irish Bob" Murphy, the well-known TV commentator and Senior PGA Tour member from Florida. Bob was a great player, but when the Irish weather turned nasty— as is its wont— he could not abide it. He cried like a banshee. I never heard such a diatribe of whinging in all my life, before or since. When we came to the watery seventh hole that I mentioned earlier, we were facing an icy hurricane. A growling Bob asked me what club he should use. I told him to hit his driver. I do not know whether he believed me or not but after he had failed to make the carry and had put four balls in the water, he certainly did. He then asked me for his golf bag, lifted it up above his head and hurled it into the lake after the golf balls. He then had second thoughts. "I need my bag, Reilly, but you can do what you like with the (bleeping) clubs." By the time I got down to the water, however, a guy from Cork named Crosbie had beaten me to it. And there was no way he would give those clubs to me. Completely unconcerned, Bob marched off to the warmth of the clubhouse with an empty golf bag slung over his shoulder.

"Big Easy" Ernie Els

Ernie "Big Easy" Els is exactly the same off the course as he is on it. He's a real nice, very quiet guy who hates fuss and loves nothing better than to sit down with his pals to spin a few yarns and have a beer and a laugh. During the Johnny Walker Classic at Phucket in Thailand, (pronounced poo-kett) we were cooling off in the clubhouse and he asked me to go and find us a "few ice cold beers." I went off and bought a six-pack covered in refrigerated ice. Ernie then guided me into a small room at the back of clubhouse where nobody would find us and we would be left alone to chat in peace.

"Reilly, I want you to caddie for me sometime," he told me. I had the feeling that his interest was more about me being an entertaining travelling companion than about any special caddying skills that I may have possessed. Expectations of me steering him toward lower scores was not part of the consideration, I'm sure. I told him that I was otherwise "engaged" and that he was far too big a star for me; I was also too old, so I didn't see it ever happening.

Some years earlier, an American player named Mike Allen

(a winner of the Scottish Open), Ernie, and I were having a beer and a chat in the VIP lounge at Charles De Gaulle Airport in Paris. We were having such a good time, in fact, that we missed our flights. This did not faze Ernie in the slightest. He coolly arranged for the three of us to stay in the Airport Hotel overnight, at his expense, and we went our separate ways the next morning, as if nothing had happened. As we say in Ireland, Ernie Els is "cool out."

Roland "Roley" Stafford

His wife called him Roley-poley, but that was far from the truth. Roland was actually a lean-mean-golfing-machine. Like many of the U.S. professionals who come to Europe to play golf, he had the appearance of a potential world-beater. Back home, though, he was just another in the pack. A very tidy player with a "waspish," sarcastic sense of humour, I caddied for Roland at Royal Portrush during the British Seniors' Championship in 1995. Players like Roland underline how many wonderful but unknown players there are all over the United States.

Roland was a music teacher in a high school in Florida before he became a golf professional. He had a lovely rhythm to his game. Being able to appreciate, play, and compose music may have helped that. After dinner at our B&B one evening he played the piano and sang one of his own compositions. It went something like:

Practise, practise what a chore. Travel, travel, what a bore.
Hooks and slices, out-of-bounds. Three-putt greens and horrid
* rounds.*
Shot too high and missed the cut. If I'd only made that putt!
We gave up almost everything. Looking for the perfect swing.
Why do we all continue when we could be sane again.
Pack the car and off again. Maybe it's my turn to win.
After fame and fortune is our goal.
For which we gave our hearts and sold our soul.

When it's over, we can say we had a ball.
Yea!

Dave Marr

I have met many really nice people through golf, and Dave Marr was one of the nicest. He was also one of the few fellows who could out-smoke me. A former Ryder Cup captain and PGA Championship winner, he was a short, tidy hitter and a great shot-maker. He could hit the ball different heights and shapes whenever he needed to.

When I first met him he was well past his best, and in his early sixties. He came to Ireland to play in the Irish Seniors Open at Shandon Park Golf Club in Belfast. But he was primarily over here to commentate for the BBC at the World Match-Play tournament at Wentworth a week later. Dave had the heaviest, most uncomfortable golf bag that I ever had the misfortune to carry. It was an ancient ceremonial Ryder Cup thing made of heavy black leather. When the bag got wet it weighed a ton. To make matters worse, the strap was much too thin and it cut into my shoulder, almost drawing blood.

In the final round we were paired with Liam Higgins, the wild Irishman from Waterville who had a good chance of winning. Liam was one of the biggest hitters you ever saw, but he never knew when or how to play safe. On the back nine, at a short but tight par 4, Higgins drew the driver. Marr nearly went apoplectic. "The man is mad!" he said out loud. Higgins ignored the illegal "advice" he was being offered and, of course, the inevitable happened: he drove it into the jungle, lost his ball and was out of the tournament.

A Scottish buddy of mine, Billy Law, used to go to the Wentworth World Match-Play event every year. If I were available, he would invite me over for a few days of R&R and to be his driver and yarn-teller-in-chief. So the week following the Irish Seniors at Shandon Park, I was pitched up by Billy Law and his friends (at their expense) in the

Runnymeade Hotel in Richmond, possibly the most expensive and classiest lodgings I ever had to "endure."

Early one evening I was having a coke in the bar while I waited for my friends to arrive for dinner. Since I was the driver, I was off the booze that week. To my surprise, the same Dave Marr that I had caddied for the week before walks into the bar.

"Reilly! What in tarnation are y'all doing here?"

"Arra," says I. "I always stay here when I am in London."

"Then I must have paid you too much," says he.

A bit later he told me about the cancer that was on the verge of killing him. He begged me to give up the smoking myself. I haven't done it yet but I know I should. Dave Marr died not long after our visit.

Without a doubt, he was one of the nicest people I ever met.

"The Darce"—Eamon Darcy

I do not think anybody knows how to figure out Eamon Darcy properly. During his long and illustrious career, "Darce" has had more caddies work for him—including me—than I have had hot dinners. Always an absolute perfectionist as far as his equipment was concerned, he would read the riot act if everything was not in perfect order. The slightest speck of dirt on a club and you'd be in hot water. He was forever changing and tinkering with his clubs, too. He was obsessive about it. If you put the bag down any other way than gently, he'd be over like a shot to see if there were any nicks on the club heads. Very few caddies could live with such tyranny for long. The fact that he has never had to pay a penny for equipment does not appear to enter his head.

One day he was walking down the first fairway with a new bagman named Frank McArdle. Eamon quickly set out his stall. "Listen, Mate (he called all his caddies Mate). I want you to know that I have a horse at home that is better bred and has more brains than you. If you remember that we will get along fine."

Another day he found a really keen and enthusiastic guy who was prepared not only to run the gauntlet of insults, but also to do the highly dangerous task of reading lines on the greens. That is a practise that is the cause of more caddies receiving the sack than any other, I can assure you. It is something I would *never* advise and have always tried to avoid. After four successful "reads," both the player and his new caddie were charmed with each other. However the inevitable happened and my colleague got one wrong.

"I knew your luck would run out, Mate," said a dismissive Darcy, and yet another promising relationship ended in a quick severance package.

But tough and all as Darcy was, you could still drive a hard bargain with him and he would stick to it—but for that week only. You would have to renegotiate all over again the following week. That is, if you were prepared to stay with him. That's why Darcy was "sacked" by caddies more often than almost any other player that I know.

It may be a fact that Darce has the most recognisably awkward-looking swing in Europe, but there is no finer striker of a golf ball. Except for Ballesteros, he is the best I have seen with a wedge in his hands. He is always moaning about his putting and forever changing his "flat stick," but he was no slouch on the greens, either. You can chalk it down and take it to the bank that once Eamon Darcy hits the big five-o he will become a multimillionaire on the Senior Tour in America.

My first memory of him is as a gangly young fellow dressed in leathers, swishing through the big iron gates of Grange Golf Club in Rathfarnham on his Honda motorcycle, his golf clubs slung precariously over his shoulder. Back then you would never have anticipated that he would become a long-lasting and successful touring professional. He was about a 14 handicap when he was a trainee assistant in the pro shop at Grange. He then went off to Erwash Valley in

England, and a few years later came out of nowhere to finish runner-up in the British PGA Championship to none other than Arnold Palmer. In his first full season on the European Tour, he finished second in the Order of Merit. After that great beginning he never looked back.

His finest hour came at Muirfield Village in Ohio in 1987 when he sank an unbelievable downhill putt to win the Ryder Cup for Europe for the first time on American soil. Believe me, you would need to be as hard as nails to withstand the pressure of that historical moment. "Darce" proved that he was up to it.

Gay Brewer

The nicest man I ever caddied for was Gay Brewer, bar none. Of course I only worked for him once, so it might have been a deceptively "good week." But all of the other caddies who have worked for Gay say the same thing, so I feel quite justified. Brewer might be a distant relation of Eamon Darcy. The two of them swing the club with a similar "flying elbow" action that is quite individualistic. A swing like that could never be taught—it would have to be acquired genetically and developed from within.

A thorough gentleman, Gay treated me in first-class fashion and paid me really well. At the end of each tiring day, he would always accompany me for a chat and a few pints of Guinness before going off to dinner. I always appreciate that. Too many golfers are in a rush to get away after their rounds these days and do not take the time to relax, smell the flowers and, as they say in America, "visit." They should.

"The Dude"—Doug Sanders

I was engaged to work for Doug Sanders in the big annual Christy O'Connor Senior Pro-Am at Hermitage not too long after he had missed the famous putt to win the Open at St.

Andrews. I was waiting at the clubhouse for him to arrive, and when he eventually did, I received a mighty shock: Doug was dressed all in pink. Clothes, shoes, glove—even the car he arrived in was pink. His personality was every bit as colourful as his gear and we had plenty of laughs going around. Unfortunately for you, most of the stories and jokes that were told are unprintable. Crooner Bing Crosby also played in our group that day. He told the dirtiest jokes of all.

When they finished their round, the players went into the locker room to shower and change. I was hanging around outside waiting to be paid (very well, as it turned out), when a little fellow with big, sad, brown eyes asked me if I could get him Doug and Bing's autographs. I went into the locker room and found the two lads, half dressed and straddling a wooden bench. There was a bottle of bourbon sitting between them.

"A little fellow outside wants your autograph," says I to Doug.

"No problem." says he, signing the paper. I then turned to Crosby, who immediately snarled at me. "Don't you ever approach me when I am in company!"

I was rocked back on my heels but I kept my trap shut and left. On my way back outside, I signed Crosby's name on the piece of paper myself. The little kid was thrilled. To this day, he probably thinks he has Bing Crosby's autograph.

A few years later I found myself caddying for Bing's son Nathaniel. He was a former U.S. Amateur champion (1981), but I could not understand how he managed to do it. I didn't think he was much of a player, but he was a nice kid and not a bit like his father.

One morning on my way to the golf course, I saw something unusual in a nearby public playground. Nathaniel was hanging upside down with his legs inserted into a pair of suspended tyres.

"What on earth are you doing?" I asked when I reached him.

"This is good exercise for my back muscles," he replied.

I remember thinking to myself that Hollywood types *are* as nutty as fruitcakes.

In 1977, I was booked to caddie for Fuzzy Zoeller at the Kerrygold Tournament at Waterville. At the last minute, though, Fuzzy telephoned the home club professional, Liam Higgins, and withdrew, leaving me high and dry. He asked Higgins for my name and told him to tell me that I should meet him at the Open Championship the following year and that he "would make it up to me." I was disappointed but there was nothing I could do; it's a normal part of every caddie's life.

At the 1978 Open, Fuzzy failed to show again so I wrote the guy off. But when he won the Masters in 1979, as a major championship winner he would definitely be going to Royal Lytham for that year's Open. When Peter Townsend failed to make it through prequalifying I hung around the clubhouse hoping that I might find a "loose" bag. I had half an eye out for Fuzzy. If I could be there "on the spot" when he arrived, I thought I might get lucky if he was not already fixed up. After waiting for a while, I realised that there was a shortage of caddies about the place. When I asked why, I was told that the aeroplane carrying a lot of the American players had been delayed and that it was due to touch down shortly.

"Jayney," I said to myself, "*that's* where all the caddies are!" How could I have missed that bit of intelligence? Meeting the plane would clearly be the best way of catching Fuzzy. I rushed off as quickly as I could but by the time I got to the airport it was too late. Another caddie, Paul "The Singing Left Foot" Stephens, had been quicker off the mark. He had met Zoeller getting off the plane and had gone with him to his hotel in Southport. I was disgusted, not least because Stephens was famous among the caddies for "stealing" other guy's bags. I could not bear it that he was the one who had outsmarted me.

I knew that most of the players would be staying in the famous King Edward Hotel in Southport, so I decided to push my luck and head over there. After arriving, I sweet-talked the girl in reception to put me through to Fuzzy's room by telephone. When I introduced myself, Fuzzy knew immediately who I was and remembered the promise that he had made two years earlier. Our telephone conversation went something like this:

"Johnny, I have a bit of a problem," Zoeller said. "Paul Stevens met me at the airport and offered me his services. I mentioned that you might be waiting for me at the golf club but he told me that you already had a bag."

"These things happen, Mr. Zoeller," I replied. "Anyway, Stephens said that he had caddied for you regularly in Australia."

"That's not true," he said. "I've never been outside of the United States before."

"Well, Stephens has been boasting about it among the other caddies for ages." I definitely smelled blood.

"Meet me at the golf club at 10 in the morning," Fuzzy said, "and we will sort it out."

The next morning "The Foot" was really singing and getting on my nerves. He was boasting about how great it was going to be caddying for the current Masters' champion in the Open Championship. When Fuzzy's big black limousine arrived on the dot of 10 a.m., "The Foot" and myself went over to him. Zoeller shook my hand. "Glad to meet you at last, Irish John."

He then turned to Paul. "Mr. Stevens, I have never been out of the United States until this trip. I have never been to Australia. Why are you telling the other caddies that you've worked for me before? I don't like liars. Now if you don't mind, 'Irish John' is going to caddie for me because I promised him my bag two years ago. I like to keep my promises."

Naturally, I was delighted. Fuzzy was a wonderful guy to be around. He was full of chat, always whistling and joking, and he had marvellous rapport with the crowds. During one of the practise rounds he noticed a small little girl pressed up against the railings behind the tee box. He went over to her, picked her up, lifted her over the railings, and handed her a club and asked her to hit a ball for him. The crowd loved it and so did the little girl. When he handed the little one back to her mother he gave both of them a big kiss. What a showman he was!

After practise one afternoon, Fuzzy asked me to take him and his wife (who I understand was a wealthy oil heiress from Texas) shopping. We travelled in the limousine and they gave me lessons in how to spend money real fast. I was in awe of it all. They bought cashmere sweaters the same way as I would buy socks—by the dozen. While she was at it, Mrs. Zoeller bought four extra sweaters, two for my partner and two for me, which was very nice.

Unfortunately, Fuzzy did not play very well and he missed the second cut after round three. There were two cuts in those days, one after 36 holes and another after 54. He shot 78-72-79.

I never caddied for Fuzzy again, but every time I see him he greets me as if we were long-lost buddies.

"Waltz" — *Philip Walton*

I have known Philip Walton since he was 17 and he has always possessed exceptional golfing talent. Like most people, however, he has an Achilles heel: Philip hates rules and regulations and he hates fuss. If he is told he must use a certain entrance, you can be sure Waltz will find a different way to get in. He likes to do his own thing and hates being bossed. He's a simple, down-to-earth guy who likes a quiet pint and a joke and then off to bed early. I was with him one day at a swanky club in England and it became the old story of me being asked to leave because "no caddies are allowed in the clubhouse." Waltz was not about to have any of it. When he lost the argument, he upped and left with me.

"What about the banquet and prize presentation?" someone asked him.

"You can have my dinner and you can post me my cheque," was his cool reply. There was no fuss, no histrionics. He just wanted to make a point.

I caddied for him in the J.P. McManus Pro-Am at Limerick Golf Club in 1995, which turned out to be his best year on tour. He was cock-of-the-walk because he had beaten Colin Montgomerie in a play-off for the English Open at the Forest of Arden only a week earlier. That victory had clinched his place on the Ryder Cup team for the matches at Oak Hill and the Limerick crowd was delighted for him. But Waltz hated all the fuss and attention that the victory had brought with it. He could not stand so many people wanting a piece of him.

"Let's get out of here, Reilly, and find a quiet pub where nobody will know us."

Not for the first or last time, we found ourselves in Pat Collins's pub in the beautiful County Limerick village of Adare. Waltz was in hog heaven because nobody paid the slightest attention to us. Pat Collins made sure of it.

A big banquet for the players and their wives was to be held that evening at Mr. McManus's mansion. A bus would collect everyone at the hotel at 7 o'clock. At 7:30, Waltz and I were still sitting in the pub. He was still wearing his golf shoes.

"You'd better get out of here or your missus will kill you!" says I. "You're dead late."

Reluctantly, Walton left his safe haven of tranquillity. His wife was waiting at the hotel door, all dolled up and ready to go, but the bus had already left. She proceeded to administer a deserved tongue-lashing, but it was like water off a duck's back. Waltz calmly shrugged his shoulders, went upstairs, showered, changed, and called a taxi. They arrived in plenty of time for the banquet.

Later that year, Waltz was one of the European heroes during the Ryder Cup matches at Oak Hill. Afterward, he admitted to me that he was so overcome by the pressure that he could not remember a thing about the last two holes that he played so bravely. He was operating entirely on automatic pilot. Furthermore, the joyous aftermath and all the fuss that was made of him back home in Ireland was far too much for

him. I believe he has subconsciously allowed his game to slip
since then because, deep down, he never again wanted to be
put in such a pressurised situation. All that Ryder Cup
hoopla is not Waltz's style. It takes the hind of an elephant, a
silicon mind, and a monumental ego to be able to cope with
all of that pressurised stuff.

I have never been directly involved in the Ryder Cup
matches myself, but the players who have say it is worse than
playing in the Open Championship. If that is the case, I am
glad I was never a part of it.

Seve Ballesteros

During the vast majority of my caddying career, Severano
Ballesteros of Spain bestrode the European golf scene like a
colossus. There was an aura of invincibility about him most
of the time. On top of that, he was a magician with a golf
club. He had to be, because of some of the unpleasant places
into which he hit his golf ball. More often than not, though,
Seve was able to conjure up an escape route and the rest of us
stood there shaking our heads in wonder.

The first time that I had a glimpse of what Seve could do
was in Germany. He was a fiery 18-year-old who spoke very
little English. On one hole, after he drove his ball into a fairway trap with a high lip on it, I took careful note of what he
would do next. He was 190 yards from the green, which was
hidden behind a line of tall trees. It seemed nearly impossible to fly a ball over the trees but Seve went into the trap
with what looked suspiciously like a 2-iron.

"What's he doing?" a startled Peter Townsend asked me.

"I haven't a clue," says I, every bit as puzzled.

Just about the next moment, Seve's ball came whizzing
out of the trap like a cannon shell. Somehow moving right to
left, the ball flew around the trees and onto the green.
Nobody watching had ever seen anything like it before, and
it was the main talking point among the caddies and players

for the rest of the week. Every one of his fellow competitors took a look at the shot that Seve had faced and every one of them shook their heads in disbelief.

Seve has an imperious nature that is hard to take sometimes. And if things are not going to his liking, he would have you believe that the whole world is against him. But he also has the common touch, as well as a marvellous sense of humour when he feels like it. He calls me "The Legend" and always greets me like a long-lost brother. During his career, Seve went through caddies like a hot knife through butter, blaming them and practically everyone else for his own mistakes. Nothing was ever his fault. Much as I admired him, it was always from a safe distance and I was never tempted to try to work for him. He would have been too hard to please.

In spite of his toughness, there is a soft side to Seve. I've had a close-up view of the guy's humanity more than once. In order to get Seve from Dublin Airport to the Spawell Golf Centre in time to participate in the tournament I arranged in aid of the blind, I was able to organise a special motorcycle escort for him through the good offices of my Dublin Garda friends, Monsell and Harrington. Seve enjoyed every minute of it and he was very appreciative. After that little bit of "rank-pulling," he kidded me about becoming his full-time "manager."

Except for many of the unfortunates who carried his golf bag, Seve always seemed to have an affinity with the caddying fraternity in general. Like many of the Spanish players, Seve came from more humble beginnings than most of the English, Irish, Australians, South Africans and Swedes on tour. Coming into golf via the caddie ranks was the traditional route in Spain and South America. Because of this, they empathised with caddies better than other players. Seve's own current bagman, however, was always excluded from any mercy, tolerance, and understanding. Anytime I was in his company he treated me with nothing but courtesy while at the same time he was giving his own caddie a hell of a time!

Tour caddies are treated quite decently in Spain. At Puerto

de Herreiro in Madrid one year, the caddies had their own comfortable dining facilities inside a large, well-appointed tent. Even better, the same food and wines were available to us at a fraction of the cost that the members and competitors were being charged in the clubhouse.

Unfortunately, the less affluent players soon found out about our bargain arrangements and began coming into our "space." Eventually there were so many players in there that the caddies were being squeezed out. Somehow Seve heard about what was happening. He did not make any direct comment, as far as I know, but the following day not one player was seen anywhere near the caddie "shack." I'm certain that Seve did something behind the scenes and the matter was sorted. That was the Seve that I admired so much. He had the ability to get things done—on *and* off the course.

Looking back over my career, Seve was the most charismatic, exciting player that I ever saw in action.

Jack Nicklaus and the "Reverend" Pat Bates

I am quite sure that if Pat Bates, the American tour pro, ever reads this he will be highly flattered to see himself getting joint billing with the great Jack Nicklaus. The "Reverend" will certainly remember (although Nicklaus might not) a practise round that Bates played with Jack and two of his sons at Castel Gondolfo in Italy. It was the one and only time that big Jack played in a European Tour event—apart from the Open, of course. The reason for this state of affairs was because it was the inaugural tournament at a course that Jack designed (in the middle of an extinct volcano, of all places). Nicklaus was present to help promote the event and the facility.

I was caddying for Pat Bates who, in addition to being a good player, was known as one of the U.S. Tour's prime Bible thumpers, or "sky pilots." That meant that he attended regular Bible-reading get-togethers with the likes of Bernhard

Langer, Payne Stewart, and Steve Jones. Pat was a very nice young man because of, or in spite of, his devotion to scripture.

As a full-time caddie, I had two great ambitions. One was to "win" the Open. The other was to someday caddie for Jack Nicklaus. I didn't achieve either of them, unfortunately, but I have been in Nicklaus's company a number of times and did get to know him quite well. I can tell you he was always extremely warm and friendly, full of chat and anecdotes and most pleasant at all times. Back in the old days, the great Jimmy Dickinson usually caddied for Jack whenever he came to Europe. To be honest, Jimmy was always as nervous as a cut cat and I don't know how Jack put up with him. Jimmy would be unable to eat for weeks before the Championship because he worried so much about it. His tummy would be in knots. Nicklaus would become something of a nursemaid to him instead of the other way around. I supposed that Jack simply liked to have Jimmy by his side and that was the key to their long-lasting relationship. At one point, Jack even moved Jimmy to Ohio and established him as the first caddie master at Muirfield Village. But Jimmy never really got settled in the USA and eventually went home to Scotland.

Anyway, when Gordon Brand Jr. and Mark Mouland saw that I was caddying for Bates in this tournament in Italy, each bet me £5 that I would not be able to get through the round. Since I didn't know much about Bates at the time, this made me apprehensive. I didn't know what to expect, but I soon found out.

On the practise putting green, Bates asked for half a dozen balls so he could mark them before we began. When he handed them back to me, I saw how he had "marked" them and a curse word slipped out before I could stop it. In an attempt to recover, I quickly asked, "What sort of mark is this? I've never seen anything like it before."

"I should warn you, John," Bates says, "that under no circumstances will I tolerate bad language. Now, what you see there is the psalm of the day. That is how I mark my golf balls."

I knew then why Brand and Mouland thought I'd have a tough time caddying for Pat.

As it turned out, the three Nicklauses and Bates and I got on famously. We had a lovely round and not one word was spoken out of place by anyone. Later, I duly collected my fivers from Gordon and Mark. The next day we had another bet—"double or quits"—that I would not last out the week.

On the final day of the tournament, Bates played very well. When we got to the sixteenth hole, he had an outside chance of winning. Needing to play a long second shot over a lake to "force" a birdie, I advised him against it but he said he wanted to have a go. The shot did not come off, unfortunately, and we were both crestfallen. As we walked down the last fairway, now with no chance at victory, Bates turned to me with a broad smile on his face.

"I sure made a right %#*&$#% of that, didn't I, Johnny?"

I laughed my arse off.

Paul "McGinty" McGinley

Following that practise round with the Nicklauses and Pat Bates at Castel Gondolfo, the five of us were sitting in the clubhouse having lunch when I spotted young Paul McGinley all alone on the far side of the room. Now, Paul is the biggest namedropper you ever did meet. He "collects" celebrities. Mind you, it would never even cross his mind that he is considered a celebrity back home in Ireland. Paul, though, has always been a great travelling companion of mine and the best of company. I knew he was having a fit watching me sitting with the Nicklauses, so I said to Jack, "That is young Paul McGinley over there on his own. He is one of the best young golfers in Ireland. May I invite him over to sit with us?"

"Certainly," Jack said. "No problem."

When I waved Paul over, you never saw anyone move so fast. He was sitting like a small puppy dog next to Nicklaus

Paul McGinley with the IPGA Championship trophy he won at Fota Island in 1997.

before you could say "Paddy McGinty's goat!" Jack, of course, continued on being pleasant, telling stories about some of his most satisfying wins. The man has an astonishing memory, and can remember in detail the shots that he played and his preshot thought processes from over 30 years ago. Before he left, Jack promised Paul that they would play a round together sometime and I know for sure that that promise was kept.

"McGinty" (that's what I call him) was always a bit of a joker, so you had to watch him like a hawk. Most of his little tricks were harmless, but nobody likes to be "caught"—least of all McGinley. So, if you happened to "get" him, he would not rest until he paid you back. We were in Jersey once, playing at La Moye. My man Des Smyth and Paul were both in contention to win. There was a long wait on the tee at the short fourteenth hole. I was not paying much attention to anything when McGinty all of a sudden asked me to get him a bottle of water. I should have been more alert, of course, and questioned why he did not ask his own caddie to do it, but I didn't. Off I trotted. By the time I got back, Paul had tied the bottom of my golf bag to the ropes that surrounded the tee and separated the spectators from the players. When it was time to go, I could not get Smythie's bag to go with me. I pulled and I tugged, and eventually brought down the entire fence of rope. McGinty roared but Smythie was not impressed. He gave us a severe dressing-down and asked the pair of us if we could be serious for five minutes. All was forgiven when Des held on for a tense, hard-earned victory.

McGinley was also involved in the accident that ended my caddying relationship with Des Smyth, albeit unwittingly. I was staying with him, Darren Clarke, and Philip Walton in a basement apartment in Spain. It was a Monday and the practise round had been abandoned because of a torrential rain. (Is there ever any other kind in Spain?) With nothing to do and bored, we four went out on the town. Believe me, there are no better guys for letting their hair down and enjoying themselves than this foursome. We were in good form when we got home that night but by no means drunk and out of control. After all the rain, the steep steps down to our apartment (they were made of railroad ties) were like sheets of ice. I was carrying one of Darren Clarke's cases and it was very heavy. Suddenly I slipped and fell, knocking McGinley over like a skittle. The two of us went down about 20 feet. I hit the deck first, and then the case and McGinley both fell on top of me. I was poleaxed, unable to move a muscle. Darren lifted me up like a small child and carried me into the bedroom. The guys put me to bed and gave me a stiff glass of whiskey to help numb the pain. The next morning I was worse, totally paralysed. An ambulance was called and I was taken to a hospital in Malaga.

I want you to know that the European Tour officials who

took over my care at that point were wonderful. They could not do enough for me, especially Carmel Treacy, an Official Recorder and staff member. After a couple of uncomfortable days, it was decided that I should be sent home on a stretcher. That trip was eventful as well because the guy beside me on the plane had a heart attack and passed away.

Back in Dublin I was put into the Mater Hospital for what seemed like an eternity. I had broken not only my wrist but two vertebrae. It took me a long time to get upright again, but Waltz, McGinty, and Clarkie were marvellous during that tough spell. They really helped me through. I will be forever grateful to them.

Darren "The Flexible Giant" Clarke

I believe it was George Bernard Shaw, a fellow Irishman, who said "the Irish are a very fair people—they never speak well of one another." Therefore, it could well be another dose of typical Irish begrudgery when I hear so many of our fellow countrymen criticising Darren Clarke for being an under-achiever. I suppose it could be a backhanded compliment that people think he should be doing better, but it also shows a severe lack of understanding of how tough it is to get to the top of the golf profession. To lampoon Darren Clarke in this way is grossly unfair and it shows a complete misunderstanding of reality. Give me a break. As I write this, the guy is ranked in the World's Top 10!

People who never met or do not know the guy personally have the cheek to say that he is lazy and that he has a chip on his shoulder. Nothing could be further from the truth. Equating an appearance of being overweight to being physically lazy is hogwash. I can tell you from my own observation of Darren day in and day out in his office (i.e. the practise ground) that he works as hard as anybody on Tour and has always done so. Butch Harmon would have nothing to do with him if he did not work his socks off. Period. I can also

tell you that he has by far the most flexibility of all the Irish
Tour players, overweight or not. His flexibility is the main
source of his natural power, technical ability, and exceptional
talent. Even fitness fanatics like Harrington and Smyth cannot match Clarke's flexibility. Big Darren undoubtedly likes
his grub but he is such a prodigious ball whacker on the
"peegee" (practise ground) that it is no wonder he has a
healthy appetite. That big engine of his needs to be topped
up with a lot of fuel.

As regards the so-called chip on his shoulder, I think that
stems from two incidents. First, his refusal a number of years
ago to wear a green sweater in the Dunhill Cup matches. And
secondly, his absence from the Irish Professional Close
Championship for a couple of years. Both are complete mis-
understandings of the reality of being a professional golfer.

The sponsor's sweaters that were given to the players to
wear at the particular Dunhill Cup in question were as heavy
as duvets. They were silk lined and as warm and cumbersome
as electric blankets. Darren simply found them too heavy,
too warm, and uncomfortable. The colour was incidental. In
fact, he did wear green that week but not the same brand of
sweater as his teammates. I saw several players cutting the
lining out of their sweaters in order to make them tolerable
to wear. Besides, when Darren was an amateur he was as
proud as anybody to "wear the green." Darren's best friends
on tour are the other Irish guys, especially Harrington and
McGinley; they all played on Irish amateur teams together
and have remained supportive of each other through thick
and thin. In addition, Darren travels and rooms with Paul
McGinley on a regular basis — they even live next door to
each other at Sunningdale and are forever visiting one
another's houses when they are at home. Darren has a fitness
room in his loft and McGinley loves to use it.

Darren's failure to play in his national championship more
often than he has was due to a contractual and management
decision and more than likely it was out of his hands. A guy

cannot be in two places at once and very few of us would show up to work for less money than that which might be available elsewhere. That is what being a professional means: you play for money and the more of it, the better!

Clarkie likes to earn money but he also likes to give it away and is an unbelievably generous guy. Harrington told me that when they were amateurs playing for Ireland, the boys on the team would often have a "whip around" for the restaurant staff members who served their table. Fellows would give what they could afford. £1, 50p, or whatever. "Big D" always threw in a fiver. His teammates thought he was mad because he was no more wealthy than the rest of them. That is just the way he was and he remains so to this day. He is never tight or shy about sharing his money.

When I was at home recovering my strength after my accident in Spain, Darren called and said that he wanted me to caddie for him during a company day (outing) at the Grange Golf Club near my home. I told him I could not even *walk* the course, let alone pull a trolley. And carrying a golf bag was completely out of the question. But he insisted on sending a taxi to my home to collect me.

"We cannot have 'Irish John' turning into a recluse," he said.

When I got to the golf club, I was astonished to learn that that he really did want me to caddie for him. He handed me the smallest golf bag I ever saw, and there were no more than half a dozen clubs in it. One of the organisers questioned the use of such a small arsenal but he was gently told that that was all that he would need to play the course. Anyway, I managed to walk nine holes but I was flattened when I finished. Darren had his tournament bag brought out to him and a reserve caddie took over so that he could complete the round. I proceeded to the clubhouse and was entertained by some old friends that I had not seen for a long time. When Darren came in, we had a few pints of Guinness together before he handed me a more-than-adequate fee for my puny "services." Nobody told him to do that and I certainly did not ask him for anything. He knew that I needed the money, however, and that getting out onto a golf course again would be good for me. That is the Darren Clarke that I know and love (although he will probably kill me for making this private matter public).

Whenever we were waiting at an airport, Darren was always the first to invite the caddies into the players' company and he would pick up the tab for any food or drink that we consumed. None of the caddies could ever afford to buy much of anything for Darren, but he sure looked after all of us in a first-class fashion.

******

The political situation in Northern Ireland has always puzzled me, but I can tell you this: the golf followers in NI are the best in the world. They turn up in numbers everywhere and they make their presence felt with their keen knowledge and enthusiasm. They also support their favourites—whether they are from the north or the south of Ireland—with great dedication and enthusiasm. Darren is of that stock, so I salute him and them.

Nobody gives you anything soft in golf. Darren Clarke is a millionaire several times over and is right at the top of the tree in world golf. He has done it all through his own talent and hard work. He comes from a humble background but he has charming parents whom I am glad to know well. They have reared a generous and loving son who now has a beautiful wife and two fine sons of his own. They should be very proud that he is willing to spread his wealth around and allow some of those less well-off than himself have a crack at it. If he believes in enjoying his money, I say more power to him.

Jimmy Heggarty, John McHenry, John O'Leary and Papwa Sewgolum

I caddied for so many professional golfers it is impossible to name them all. I would like to mention a few, though, such as Jimmy Heggarty from Portrush who was Des Smyth's best pal on tour for 15 years. I caddied for Jimmy off and on, and he was a fine little player. Unfortunately, like so many players who nearly made it, he was not quite good enough. The tell-tale sign to me was the fact that he carried a 3-iron, which he never, ever used. It was always "a wee-cut four wood" for Jimmy. I used to tell him to take that 3-iron out of his bag and introduce something more useful, such as an extra wedge. But every time I looked into his bag, there was that spotless club sitting there waiting for a chance at glory.

******

For a short spell at the very end of my career, I caddied for John McHenry from Cork. John and I very nearly won the Irish Open at Mount Juliet but he could not find that extra gear on Sunday and the pack of pursuers swallowed us up. John was a really nice guy and a thorough gentleman. In my opinion, though, he was too nice for the cutthroat business of being a professional athlete. Seriously, he would nearly apologise if he sank a chip or a long putt. McHenry struck the ball beautifully and worked as hard as anyone but he was too nervous, too conservative in his approach and—most important of all—too poor a putter to reach the heights that his ball-striking ability deserved. I felt that John was as accurate as Langer with his irons. For some reason, however, he would never attack the flag. He always went for the fat of the green. If he had gone directly at the target more often, I believe it would have taken the pressure off his putting.

The last Irishman to win the Irish Open was John O'Leary, my fellow Dubliner. O'Leary was a superb, stylish player who was good enough to play on the GB&I Ryder Cup team in 1975. He was always a bit of a rogue, good fun to be with, and he was very generous to all of us caddies. There was always a scramble to be allowed to carry John's bag. Whenever he did particularly well in a tournament and made a good cheque, there would be a queue of caddies waiting for him, looking for a "loan." John was a bit of a "softie" but he was no fool. You could get a dropsy off him, maybe twice, but that would be the end of it.

He was a colourful character with his Afro hairstyles and outrageous outfits, but he was also capable of winning the Open Championship. Unfortunately, he suffered from a bad back and eventually it put a premature end to his career. Ultimately, he became a headquarters official with the European Tour and is currently on the Ryder Cup Committee.

I am proud to say that I had the distinction of caddying for the first black man to play on the European Tour. His name was Papwa Sewgolum and he was a South African Indian. I "picked him up" rather by accident at Woodbrook in the Carroll's Tournament. Papwa ended up playing all four rounds, which was quite an achievement considering the limitations that were put on his golf game back home. He played "cack handed" (the left hand below the right) and this attracted a lot of interest in Ireland because there are a large number of club golfers with hurling* backgrounds who play the same way. At one point, Papwa told me he did not like the cold and could not wait to get back to Africa. My guess is that he won enough money in one season in Europe to keep him going for several years at home and it was another reason why he did not bother to return.

*Hurling is the national game in Ireland. It is played at great speed with a ball and a stick by teams of 15 players. It could be described as "aerial field hockey" and is a game of high skill.

"The Shark" — *Greg Norman*

I have been told more than once that if I put on one of those hats that Greg Norman wears and similar clothes, I would pass for a reasonable, if more elderly, smaller imitation of the Shark himself. Be that as it may, Paul McGinley has a younger sister, Susanne, who I am sure is a fine young woman today. When she was still a youngster, Susanne had a severe crush on the "Great White Shark." Absolutely besotted by Mr. Norman. A few years ago, Greg came to County Kilkenny to play in the Irish Open at Mount Juliet. Hearing of this visit, Miss McGinley pestered her big brother to get her an autographed photograph. He "kindly" referred her to me.

"Uncle Johnny's the man if you want an autographed photo," Paul told her. "He'll get it for you." He then disappeared onto the practise ground, literally leaving me holding the baby. My young friend and I went in search of the Shark and found him on the chipping green. He was quite a bit away from the clubhouse but was surrounded by a horde of enthusiastic fans. It was an impossible situation and I knew that under these circumstances the brush-me-off was inevitable.

But as I looked into Susanne's bright, excited eyes, I grew courage and strength. Greg and I knew each other from his early days on the European Tour, plus he had been involved in a recent episode that I had when I was in Australia, which I will now tell you about.

Smythie and Ronan Rafferty were playing for Ireland in the World Cup near Sydney, so Ben Dunne and his wife generously took me along with them for a bit of a holiday. Australia is a fantastic country; I saw Darling Harbour and my first kangaroo. I also met a lot of Irishmen, including

Who else but The Shark, Greg Norman.

some far distant relations. I had a marvellous time and took some great photographs. The first day that we went to the tournament, however, my camera was stolen from beside the putting green and I was very upset about it. After somebody told Greg Norman what had happened, he proceeded to go on Australian TV and publicly berated the thief for besmirching the reputation of the Australian people.

"Is this the way to treat visitors to our country?" growled Greg into the camera.

Well, guess what? It worked! The next day my camera was "found" in the exact spot from which it was taken. A note of apology was with it, and the film was intact too. That was of greater interest to me than the camera. Anyhow, I now hoped that that incident would somehow help me get a photo for my little friend.

I told Susanne to stay put and I went under the ropes and approached Norman. He was not at all pleased to see me coming because I'm sure he knew that he was going to be asked to do another favour.

"Whatever it is, Johnny," Greg said, "if I do it for one I will have to do it for them all. I'll be stuck here all day!"

"'Tis a terrible price to pay for fame and fortune," I replied sarcastically. "Look, Greg, it's Paul McGinley's little sister we are talking about. If I bring her over here, you'll be safe from the crowd."

"Oh, all right, let's do it. But hurry up."

I took the photo with Susanne's camera and, if I do say so myself, it turned out to be a gorgeous picture of the pair of them. Naturally, Susanne was thrilled.

It took a couple of days for the photo to be developed and enlarged. After she brought it back to me, it was then my task to get it autographed. Luckily, it all worked out fine. Greg was perfectly gracious when I found him in the club-house after his round. He autographed the picture, no trouble at all, and I am told that it hangs in the young woman's bedroom to this day.

"Pawdrigg" Harrington (1996 to 1998)

Padraig Harrington was standing with his hands on hips in the middle of the fifteenth fairway of the Club de Campo golf course in Madrid. It was the final round of the 1996 Spanish Open, and we were leading. Harrington was a young rookie, a tour pro for a mere six weeks. He was as nervous as a kitten and it was hard to blame him. I knew it was my job to keep him calm and somehow steer him home.

"Okay, Johnny, what have we got?"

"250 to the front, 265 to the flag" says I.

"What will we do, lay up?"

"Why would you want to do that?" I replied. "You've reached the green from here the last three days. Hit the same thing again. Driver."

"Okay, boss," Padraig says. He takes a deep breath and hits

Precise calculation of every yardage is vital to the relationship between caddie and player. In this instance, Padraig is making sure I subtracted instead of added—or vice versa!

an absolute beauty, on the money all the way onto the dance floor. I am as chuffed as could be. Neither of us can hardly feel our feet under us touching the ground as we walk down the hill to that bowl-like green. A birdie would put us four in front with three to go. *Nothing will stop us now*, I thought.

Padraig duly made the two-putt birdie, and from there on he was completely relaxed and totally in control of his game and himself. That shot was the clincher. I always believe that you should not trick around and try to finesse when your back is to the wall and under pressure. Situations like those are what pros do all the practise for, so they should simply trust themselves and perform automatically.

We had been up since before 5 o'clock that morning because we had to play the last four holes of the third round and due to more heavy rain the final round was also a stop-go affair. A couple of times it looked as if the whole thing could have been called off. But we plugged on regardless. After Padraig made his par at 16, he hit his tee shot on the par-3 at 17 within 20 feet of the flagstick. With that, I handed him the putter and scrambled up the hill to the eighteenth tee. I was tired, my back was killing me, I needed a rest and, most of all, I needed some time to think. I had hardly sat down when I hear this almighty roar behind me. Of course, I knew what had happened.

As Padraig paraded up the hill to the tee with that jaunty sailor's gait of his, I said, "Good birdie, P!"

"How did you know I sank the putt?" he asked. "You weren't even there?"

"Do you think I am deaf?" I said with a laugh, all the while thinking of my bonus for helping him win.

A bit of care and it was all over, save the celebrating. I handed Padraig a 4-iron.

"I was thinking of the driver," he said. "I can easily fly those traps."

"No way, Padraig. We are not taking any chances at this stage. Even with a double bogey you might still win by a couple of shots, but let's not find out. Hit the 4- iron."

He did, and it was perfectly placed in the middle of the fairway. A solid 8-iron uphill and onto the elevated green meant that after only six weeks on tour we had won a really big one, the Spanish Open. Padraig three-putted for bogey but it did not matter because he was well clear. It was almost dark when we finished and I had never been so tired. I did not even think of celebrating and neither did he. Padraig does not drink anyway. A real sound kid, he is.

After the presentation ceremony we went straight back to the hotel and fell into bed. We had an early 6 o'clock flight from Madrid the next morning. While having breakfast at the airport, I finally got a chance to pop the question. "Well, how am I fixed?"

"What do you mean?" Padraig asked.

"When we met for the first time at Spawell Golf Centre

and I agreed to caddie for you, your dad said that you would give me a six-week trial. The six weeks are up."

"Johnny," he said, "you are going *nowhere*. You are staying with me. We are going right to the top together."

Only 10 weeks earlier, I had never heard of Padraig Harrington. I was out of golf, out of work, and on the dole. I had no money or prospects and I was depending on people like Ben Dunne to take me golfing once in a blue moon and hopefully throw a few bob in my direction.

The injuries from the fall I suffered in Spain a year earlier had cost me my job because I was such a long time recuperating. If it were not for the kindness of several friends — Darren Clarke, Phil Walton, and Paul McGinley in particular — I might not have made it through. Now I was back and heading for the top with a young fellow who was one of the most dedicated and hard-working golfers I had ever seen. I felt that he was in the class of Bernhard Langer, and that is saying something. Better still, the purses had mushroomed enormously and so had the wages of caddies.

The Spawell meeting with Padraig and his father had came about when a good friend of mine, John Monsell, who is a Detective Sergeant at Tallaght, near where I live, phoned me out of the blue and asked me if I would like to go back to caddying.

"Depends on the offer," I said cagily.

Monsell asked me if I would be willing to talk to a colleague of his, Pat Harrington, and his son Padraig, whom he said had just turned professional and was looking for an experienced caddie.

"This kid is special, he is seasoned and he has the game. All he needs is a bit of experience on Tour," Monsell told me.

"There are good experiences and bad experiences," I said, showing no real enthusiasm. But I also had nothing to lose. I was at the bottom and the only way I could go was up. I agreed to talk to them.

When we met, the first thing that Harrington Senior said

to me was: "Would you like a pint?" Padraig was not a drinker, and I could not help noticing him watching the pint, and the several more that followed, disappearing. I knew very well what he was thinking. So I told him that my days of drinking more than I should were well behind me. We sat in the bar in Spawell and we went through the whole business. It took a couple of hours and quite a few more pints before we were all satisfied with the planned itinerary and my job specification. I really liked Pat. He had a wonderful laugh and a great sense of humour. Padraig was more business-like and was only interested in what I could do that would help him to play better golf.

"I will tell you stories and keep you relaxed," I said. "I've been around so often I know what is required—as good as anyone." So we struck our deal for a six-week stint and I was happy to be going back to work again.

Every time we had to go somewhere Pat Harrington would drive from Templeogue to Tallaght to collect me and bring me to the airport. Of course, he did the reverse when we came home again. It was a big improvement on the bad old days when I had to fend for myself and somehow get to the next destination via the cheapest possible means. Pat Harrington was wonderful to me, as was his lovely wife, Breda.

When we had shaken hands on our deal, I asked Padraig for a sub.

"What do you mean?" says he, puzzled.

"I have no money. Can you advance me a few quid?" He gave me 20 pounds and from that day on was always asking me if I had enough money to get myself home or whatever. He never once left me short during our three years together. It was a great arrangement, not least because I knew very early on that I was with somebody special who was going to become a superstar. How did I know that? Padraig's short game is up there with the best of them and he practised it morning, noon, and night. He is in the Bernhard Langer and

Vijay Singh class as a workaholic on the practise ground. Right from the word go he has always been completely professional in his approach to his golf, on and off the course. Nothing is ever left to chance. It is why the famous incident at the Belfry in 2000 when he marked his card incorrectly, costing himself certain victory in a big tournament, was such a surprise. I like to think that it would not have happened if I was with him on that occasion but that would not be fair to the unfortunate caddie involved. It is, after all, the player's sole responsibility.

I must admit that Padraig's attention to detail sometimes got on my nerves. On the course he could be very fussy. Pacing up and down like a soldier, walking ahead to look at a green that had not moved since the previous time that we had checked it out. All the information he needed was written in his notebook but he would not look at it. Walking forward is his way of coping with the tension of the moment and he has always done it. The Americans who said he was trying out a bit of gamesmanship on Mark O'Meara during in the Ryder Cup at Brookline were wrong. When Padraig "walked," he was just being Padraig. He was reverting to type. He was only wandering off, trying to calm down. Padraig is too straight and upright a guy to even consider trying to "bustle" an opponent.

We had three great years together. Although we did not win again until the 1997 World Cup at Kiawah Island in South Carolina, but we were in contention often. Seven second-place finishes we had. After about a year on tour, Padraig was signed up by IMG. Not long after that, I began to notice little things that were beginning to undermine our relationship. It all came to a head at the Murphy's English Open at the Forest of Arden in 1998.

Padraig was not playing well and was in danger of missing the cut. At the best of times, he's a slow player. A Rules Official put the stopwatch on him and it caused him to become irritated, which, to be fair, was not normal behaviour.

Coming down the last few holes, as soon as he found the green with his approach shot, I handed him his putter and, as I often did, went to the next tee. Padraig accused me of rushing him. Then, at the last hole, a long par 3 over water, he asked me which club he should hit.

"The 2-iron," I said.

"I was thinking of a 4," he replied.

"Are you on drugs?" I asked, showing a little impatience of my own. "You are way out."

We compromised and he hit a 3-iron. It never had a chance and it came up short in the bunker. Bogey. Missed cut. Olazabal was playing with us and he hit a *1-iron*.

"I think it is time we took a break," Padraig said to me as we left the green.

I was heartbroken, but it was not my call. I went home and instinctively tried to start a new life. Four months later Padraig telephoned me and asked me to come back and do the last four tournaments of the season with him. We got on famously and it was as if I had never been away. I knew, though, that I was finished with professional caddying. I had

had enough of traipsing around the world. The forced break had given me time to reappraise my life. And even if it had not happened, I am convinced that something else would have come up that would have driven a bit of overdue sense into my skull. I was quite glad and relieved to be finished. The IMG critics were right; I was too old.

It was time for me to go home and stay home.

Hobnobbing with Royalty

Touring professionals usually play a schedule of three or four events in a row, then take one week off. At the very height of the season they might go six weeks (especially if they're playing well) before taking a rest. Staying on tour any longer than that can turn a fellow into mush.

All those rest periods are fine for them but what about the unfortunate caddie? While the players are sorting out their games at home, or merely resting up, they forget that we have to buy food for our families and pay our rent. Unless he is raking in the winning bonuses, a caddie's weekly wage does not allow him the luxury of taking too much time off very often. Therefore, when my regular employer headed home, I would continue on to the next tournament site and try to pick up whatever stray bag might be available. There are always player/caddie teams breaking up, fellows coming and going. There are also some players in every tournament who are there because of a sponsor's invitation or because they won a qualifier. Therefore, an experienced caddie like me could often get a bag.

The many precedents of hastily cobbled together combinations do not help the potential volatility that is frequently present in a player/caddie relationship. Many players are not the slightest bit squeamish about taking on a new assistant. Golf is their livelihood , so there is little sentiment. It is also true, however, that when some caddies get the chance to take on what they think will be a more lucrative bag, they can be just as ruthless. Smythie once showed me a letter from one of my so-called "colleagues," who shall remain nameless, stating that I was much too old to be on the tour and that Des would be much better off with a younger man like him who would do a far better job. Smythie wrote back and told him that no matter how good he was, he still would not be as good as me. That should tell you a lot about Smythie's character.

During my career, I received many opportunities to caddie for others while Townsend, Smyth, and Harrington were at home doing other things. But not once did I consider ending our standing arrangements. If they were loyal to me, I was more than happy to return the compliment. I always went back to them no matter how well my "pickups" did. Sometimes, though, those extra jobs took me on the most amazing adventures.

One of the happiest and most memorable experiences I had occurred when Smythie was taking one of his furloughs. I was offered the bag of the fine Swedish player, Anders Forsbrand, at a big pro-am at Epsom RAC, an exclusive and extremely wealthy club in the middle of the stockbroker belt of southwest London. I stayed with friends in Hounslow and took a taxi to the golf course on the first day. My driver was a stern-looking Asian fellow. On arrival at the gates of the golf club I offered him a 20-pound note but he had no change. I showed my caddie's badge to the man at the players' entrance and we were allowed to go inside on the strict understanding that the taxi would come straight back out again. When we got to the front door of the clubhouse, I asked my driver to wait a minute while I went to the bar for change. I jumped out of the car, flashed my badge at the doorman and before he could blink, I was past him and inside. The taxi driver must have thought I was going to cheat him out of a hard-earned fare because he jumped out of the cab and headed after me screaming and cursing. He only got as far as the threshold before he was unceremoniously stopped by a solid scrum of security guards. The poor fellow created an enormous commotion, bawling and shouting his head off. Fortunately, it did not take me long to get the necessary change, much to the relief of the frantic taxi driver. "I thought you were going to do a bunk on me, mate," he said.

"No way," says I. "Give every man his due."

When I tried to get back into the clubhouse again, a big burly rugby type with an unbelievable Oxbridge accent stopped me in my tracks. The guy was wearing a big red rosette like the ones you would see being given out at the Dublin Horse Show. I could not take my eyes off it.

"Who are you?" he demanded.

"Even a policeman wouldn't ask me that question," I replied with a touch of indignance.

"I *am* a policeman," he said, continuing to block my way.

I thought to myself, *What am I going to do now?* I was having no success talking my way past this formidable barrier when Eamon Darcy came along.

"What's the problem, Reilly?" asks Darce, with a big grin on his face. "Do they think you are after the crown jewels?"

I explained the difficulty I was having.

"Johnny is all right," Eamon told the guard. "He's with me. I'll take care of him."

Only then—but clearly reluctantly—did the security man allow me to enter the Epsom RAC clubhouse. I went into the dining room to look for Anders and saw him sitting at a table with a group of about half a dozen people. I made sure he saw me but waited for him to beckon me over. You can call that caddie protocol or just good manners. At last he waved me over but did not formally introduce me to each member of the group. He simply said, "This is 'Irish Johnny,' my caddie."

Knowing my place, I duly sat down but did not say anything. I was still thinking about the security guard and only half-listened to the chitchat back and forth. Eventually, though, my curiosity got the better of me.

"Tell me, please, what's all the big security about? The guy at the door is very jumpy."

Anders laughed. "It is all about the guy sitting beside you," he said, "and it is going to be a lot worse when we get onto the golf course because we are playing with him." Everyone at the table seemed to think this was amusing. I looked at the bloke to my left but did not have a clue who he was.

"Who are you," I asked, "that you need so much security?"

The fellow put on the most beautiful smile and began to chuckle. "I'm Andrew," he said, "Duke of York."

I was so embarrassed. Truly, I could have jumped into the hole on the eighteenth green nearby. Prince Andrew was really lovely about my lack of awareness, however. He didn't seem to mind one little bit that I did not recognise him. Very down to earth, he was. Once we got onto to the golf course, I began telling HRH a few of my stories. We got along wonderfully. During a long wait, I shoved a scorecard at him and asked him for his autograph. He said he was sorry but he couldn't do it. Royal protocol, it seemed, did not allow him to sign anything. I asked him if he would pose for a photograph instead. Again, he said he couldn't.

"I am not allowed to do that, either, without the prior permission of Buckingham Palace."

"What *are* you allowed do?" says I, laughing.

"Not much," he said with a smile. "I receive my instructions every morning. Where I have to go and what I have to do and what I am supposed to say."

"Janey, your Highness," I said. "That is no life at all."

"Sometimes, I think you are right, Johnny. There are times when I would love to be a caddie just like you. Or even better," he said wistfully, "a tournament player like Anders."

"Are you allowed to have a pint?"

Prince Andrew laughed. "Oh, yes. That I can. And I hope you will join me after the game for at least one, and you can continue telling me your fascinating stories."

"Ah, your Highness, they won't allow me in there at all."

"Oh yes, they will!" he said. "As soon as we have finished and you have taken care of Anders's things, put on your best bib and tucker and I will send one of my bodyguards to escort you to my private room. We will continue our chat and have a few beers. I love your Irish blarney!"

Prince Andrew was an excellent 6-handicap player, and judging by his display that day was well able to account for himself on the golf course in public, unlike many amateurs who would be overwhelmed. The crowds did not seem to bother him in the slightest. His royal training obviously stood him in good stead in that regard. The Prince told me that a former touring pro named Doug McClelland was his personal golf coach and teacher. Doug has certainly done a fine job. I am sure the Duke could play to scratch if he was able to spend more time at the game, without having to deal with all of the hoopla.

Inside the clubhouse later that day, I told HRH a story that I hope he repeated the next time he saw his aunt, Princess Margaret. I was once waiting for a connection in the railway station in Paris and I had Peter Townsend's bag with me. This Frenchman comes up to me, points at the bag and in faltering English asks me for an autograph. I tried to explain that I was only a caddie and not the person he thought I was. But he was a persistent so-and-so and would not take no for an answer. When I realised he did not understand a word I was saying, and the only way to get rid of him was to oblige, I signed "Peter Townsend" with a flourish. It didn't work, however, because he continued trying to engage me in conversation, none of which made any sense to me. Gradually it dawned on me that the guy thought I was the

Peter Townsend who was once engaged to Princess Margaret, the Queen of England's sister. At that point I knew I was out of my depth, so I vamoosed.

About 15 months after the Epsom pro-am I was caddying for Smythie in the British Open at Royal Birkdale, the one that "the Hyphen" (Ian Baker-Finch) won. There was a mixed group of caddies, players, and wives standing at the corner of the unique white clubhouse, all enjoying the atmosphere and watching the players finishing on the eighteenth green. U.S. Tour player Freddie Couples and his wife were standing right beside me. Suddenly, Freddie, who is normally a very laid-back guy, became a bit animated and said, "There is Prince Andrew coming toward us. I'd love to meet him."

And sure enough, here comes the Prince up this path, shaking hands and exchanging pleasantries with the spectators. Suddenly, he sees me. A broad smile comes over his handsome face and—totally ignoring everybody else—he greets me like a long-lost brother. "Johnny, it has been a while. How are you keeping?"

Well, the Couples's jaws nearly hit the floor. Believe me, they were flummoxed. Naturally, I introduced Prince Andrew to them—which pleased them very much. I must admit, though, that I was pretty pleased myself that the Duke remembered me.

"Reilly," Freddie's wife said after HRH had left, "how do you know royalty?"

"'Tis a long story," says I.

Behind the Iron Curtain

Most ordinary mortals would think that the ordeal I under-
took to get to New Zealand was enough hardship for one
lifetime, but if you were a dedicated touring caddie like me,
such adventurous journeys were easy enough to match. Now
I must admit that my extraordinary trip to Berlin in the early
1970s occurred when I was a strong and determined young
buck capable of enduring almost any hardship and discomfort.
But when I think back on what I had to go through to make
the first tee at the 1975 German Open and what followed
afterward, I realise that it was no wonder that my hair turned
grey prematurely.

In 1975, I had only just begun caddying full-time for Peter
Townsend, the Ireland-based Englishman, and I probably
had not yet figured out how to combat both the temptations
and boredom of overseas travel. Townsend used to pay me an
agreed retainer at the beginning of each tournament week
and then a percentage of his purse at the end. When the
German Open came up on our schedule (in Berlin), I began

my journey by travelling on the overnight ferry across the Irish Sea from Dublin to Liverpool. Once I discovered that there was a blackjack game on the boat, instead of taking "forty winks," I stupidly stayed up all night and lost all of my money. I still had to get to Berlin, but I hadn't a penny.

After arriving in Liverpool, quite brazenly and without the slightest idea of how I was going to complete the trip, I boarded the train to Southampton. With the ticket collector getting too close for comfort, I had a mean and nasty brain-wave and decided to take a different kind of gamble. When I saw a fellow going into a nearby toilet, I knocked on the door and shouted, "Tickets" in my best "scouser" (Liverpudlian) accent. The poor guy shoved his ticket under the door and I ran off with it. That got me to Southampton without further incident but it was only the easy part—now we had to catch the ferry to Holland. With that major task in mind, one of my caddie friends got onto the boat and immediately made an excuse that he had to get off again. He was given a pass. He then gave it to me and talked his way back on again by insisting that they had not given him a pass in the first place. It worked, so I was now able to get to the Hook of Holland without any further heart strain. When we arrived in Holland, the next leg of the journey to Berlin was by express train. What made this part of the trip complicated was the fact that we had to briefly pass through the Iron Curtain and enter Communist East Germany. That meant that our tickets, visas, and passports would be closely scrutinised. By this time, our group of travelling Irish caddies had been reinforced by a number of our English colleagues and everyone became switched on by the challenge of getting me to Berlin. Trying to beat the system has always been a stimulating endeavour for travelling caddies.

The plan we came up with called for me to be put into a golf bag cover and then lifted up onto the overhead rack. I was up there inside in that bag for several hours without even a drink of water. When the security people came around to stamp passports, I held my breath until they moved on.

After they left, I jumped out of the bag, grabbed my pass-port, borrowed an already stamped train ticket, and ran after the policemen. To one of them, I said, "You punched my ticket but you forgot to stamp my passport."

He looked at me suspiciously, long and hard, and I had visions of a firing squad. But suddenly he smiled broadly and stamped my passport. I had made it through to Berlin and, more importantly, would be able to get back out again. Believe me, you would have thought that that would have been quite enough excitement for one week.

But it was far from it.

The tournament in Berlin was to be played on a golf course belonging to and attached to a U.S. Army base. All the caddies were housed in a disused wooden army billet behind the clubhouse, where we slept on a mixture of hammocks and stretchers. We were given instructions to keep the place clean and tidy because during the day our dormitory was to double up as a private dressing room for Arnold Palmer and Tony Jacklin, who were the two big stars of the tournament. Arnold was highly amused by this state of affairs and had no difficulty "slumming" with a bunch of ragamuffin caddies. He even sat down and joined us in our yarn swapping. Jacklin, on the other hand, was clearly miffed about the situation— his nose very much out-of-joint. He obviously considered it beneath him to have to share space with the likes of us.

On the grounds—as at most professional golf tournaments in those days—there was a tented "village" where clothing, equipment, and other ancillary goods were displayed for marketing purposes. On the second night of the tournament, one of the tents was raided and thousands of pounds worth of merchandise was stolen. It was mostly resellable stuff such as shirts, sweaters, and golf clubs. Surprise, surprise: us vagabond caddies became the prime suspects. So the six most senior of us (Scotty Gilmour, Pete Coleman, John Graham, "South African Basil," the Scot "Blackie," and myself) were called up before the European Tour Director, Ken Schofield.

The riot act was read to us even though we did not know anything about the robbery. We were then treated like English public schoolboys and told that we were going to be made examples of: all of us would be suspended from the Tour indefinitely. It seems that we were guilty until we somehow could manage to prove our innocence. We were adamant that we had nothing to do with the crime but our protests fell on deaf ears. Therefore, the only way of proving our innocence was to find the culprits ourselves.

We had another caddie conference and decided to become private eyes and do our own detective work. Thanks to some fortunate sleuthing by John Graham, who accidentally overheard a conversation while he was behind a hedge near the practise ground, we found out that the guilty parties were two young English rookie professionals who were playing in the tournament but who had missed the cut. We immediately tipped off Schofield and when the police went to the young fellows' room they found the stolen gear.

I have to admit that touring caddies could never be accused of being paragons of virtue; as a group and as individuals we are well capable of pulling the odd dubious prank. But outright robbery would rightly be considered out-of-bounds. Scotty Gilmour and I made a compensation deal with Schofield. The six "accused" were to be reinstated forthwith and given 100 Deutsche marks each, plus some of the recovered clothing and a crate of beer. The story got better for me after Townsend had a good week and I made a nice bonus on top of all of that booty. What I should have done was gone straight home at that point, because the next phase of our German odyssey was even more unbelievable, complicated, and scary.

The European Tour staff had a bus that was used as a kind of mobile office at various sites for checking scores and other administrative duties. On the final day of the tournament in Berlin, Schofield approached me and asked me if I knew whether or not any of the caddies could drive a bus. "We need the mobile office to be driven down to Crans sur Sierre in

Due to my experience at driving a bus in my younger days, I volunteered my services under certain conditions. Ken had no objections to my demands, so I got the job. I had immediately seen the opportunity for several lucrative spin-offs. I had a free ride to Switzerland, I could pack the bus with caddies for a small fee, and I could bring the players' bags for another small fee, which would spare them the inconvenience of having to transport the bags themselves. I cut Scotty Gilmour in on the action and appointed him my chief navigator and assistant driver.

After being on the road for a few hours I became slightly uneasy. "Are you sure we are going in the right direction?" says I to Scotty.

"Of course I am, Mate," the deluded navigator replied. Suddenly—his words hardly out of his mouth—we were surrounded by a posse of police cars carrying about a dozen agitated, armed occupants. They shouted at me to pull over, which I did.

It turned out that we had somehow managed to cross over the border into East Germany and we were now heading for Czechoslovakia. All 18 of us were escorted to the nearest prison and kept under armed guard overnight. The next morning a uniformed American military policeman assigned to the United Nations arrived to interview us. After he had listened patiently to our story and had examined our passports, he said, "Jeez, Mr. O'Reilly, only an Irishman could manage to do what you have just done: you have breached some of the tightest security in the world. I have lived here for 12 years and have seen some of the most ingenious, inventive, hair-brained, and courageous schemes for getting people over that border. But you did it without even trying!"

The UN representative managed to get us released fairly promptly and we were escorted the 20 miles or so back to the border. A local train engineer (who had usurped Scotty's position as navigator) sat beside me in the bus and gave me directions while two police cars, one in front and one in back, kept an eye on our progress. The train engineer was a nice guy, so one of the lads gave him a few porno magazines. Another gave him a pair of Levi jeans and I gave him what was left of that crate of beer Schofield had given us. You would have thought it was Christmas he was so thrilled, and he thanked us over and over again in broken English. We didn't give the police anything, and they were so annoyed by this state of affairs that they refused to give the engineer a lift back home. For all I know, the poor guy had to walk all the way, carrying his presents. I have often wondered if he made it safely.

As we cruised down the autobahn toward Switzerland, with Scotty now fully reinstated in the navigator's chair, we began to smell something burning. When we stopped and looked under the bonnet, the engine was glowing as red as Rudolph the Reindeer's nose. We managed to get to a nearby garage and after a complete oil change and a new fan belt was fitted, we were on our way again. After we passed through Berne, we began the steep climb up to Crans "Montana." which is more correctly known as Crans sur Sierre. I could only drive in first gear for the last 10 miles, so it took us the best part of two hours to complete this last lap of the trip into the Alps. There was a backup of a couple of hundred cars honking crazily behind us, trying to pass, but nobody could get by. It must have been quite a sight.

The bill for fixing the bus came to a very reasonable 90 francs. But before the request for reimbursement was proffered to the European Tour Office in Switzerland, quite mysteriously an extra zero was added in the appropriate spot—for the emotional wear and tear the trip took on us poor caddies. Remembering the brouhaha in Germany, the officials did not dare question our "honesty," and we got it.

I then went to park the bus. An officious Frenchman directed me to do so on an embankment overlooking the eighteenth green so that the players would not have too far to walk before handing in their scorecards. I was very reluctant and warned him that if it rained heavily overnight the bus might slide. But the guy insisted, so I did as I was told.

It *did* rain hard during the night and my worst fears came to pass. When I got to the club the next morning, officials, players and the greenstaff were all shouting and waving their arms about and looking for a scapegoat because the bus was sitting, slightly askew, in the middle of the eighteenth green.

"Reilly," an official said to me, "why the hell did you park the bus there?"

"Because that gentleman over there," I said, pointing at the guilty Frenchman, who promptly turned as red as the engine was when we were inspecting it back on the autobahn, "instructed me to do so."

Heavy equipment was needed to get the bus off the green and back over the embankment. The putting surface was destroyed and it took a huge effort by the greenkeeping staff to make it playable again. Later, I was told to drive the bus to a nearby garage and park it. Seven years later, it was still right where I had left it. It could still be there, for all I know, and I have no idea why it was abandoned like that.

Thailand

If I am ever lucky enough to win the lottery, there is one place in the world above all others that I would choose to return to without any hesitation. And that place is Thailand. More than any of the many places that I have been to, the city of Phucket in Thailand (pronounced poo-kett) appeals to me the most for a holiday. It is so different from home; the shopping, the restaurants and the beaches are amazing. Above all, in spite of our huge cultural differences, I found the Thai people to be warm, friendly, and very nice.

In 1998, "Master" Harrington graciously brought me all the way to Phucket for the Johnny Walker Classic. Upon arriving on the Monday before the tournament, we were shown the setup of the place. It was pretty spectacular. The clubhouse was super plush and there were several swimming pools and outdoor bars. We soon found out that there were 250 caddies registered on the club's books and that all of them were little girls. I mean really little. Each one of them was about four and a half feet tall and all giggles. They were

I appear fairly relaxed before I embarked on the most terrifying experience of my life—a ride through the streets of Phucket, Thailand, in 1998 on the back of this enormous elephant!

lovely, always happy and smiling and willing to help their visitors. They had their own excellent quarters, a "caddie shack" that would put facilities even in the United States to shame. All the girls dressed in full-length coats or gowns and wore wide-brimmed hats as protection from the extremely hot sun.

When we arrived for our first practise round, there were half a dozen of these girls waiting on the first tee. Believe it or not, a few of them were there to carry the golf bags for the other visiting caddies and me. Now that was certainly a first. And you should have seen those little four and half-foot girls shouldering those big tournament bags! It was no bother to them, no bother at all. Each group also had a girl carrying a stool and umbrella in case anybody needed to sit down under a shade and rest for a while. Another girl carried a trowel and bucket of sand and grass seed for repairing divots. Another little one carried the drinks. We were like a small parade going down the fairways. The girl who carried my bag was a lovely little thing named Phum. She did not speak any English but she seemed to understand me whenever I spoke to her.

When I returned home, I got a great kick out of telling my buddies in Molloy's Pub in Tallaght that one of the highlights of my trip to Thailand was taking an elephant ride through the streets of Phuket and eating a snake. I must admit that the elephant ride absolutely terrified me. As for the eating experience, I had to make my selection while the damned thing was asleep but still fully alive in a glass case. It was similar to selecting a lobster at home, but pretty scary, being forced to watch the execution ritual. A beheaded snake takes a long time to stop wriggling and jumping around. It was still hopping on the wok, or whatever they call it, as it was being stir-fried. I only ate it on a dare and to win a bet but I was surprised to find I quite enjoyed the taste and would willingly do it again without any incentive. I would pass on having to observe the preliminaries, though.

At the pro-am before the tournament, we were paired with Wayne "Radar" Riley from Australia. Believe me, the reason he is called Radar has *nothing* to do with straight hitting. After one of several wild tee-shots, Radar snapped his Great Big Bertha Driver over his knee and hurled the remnants into a swamp. The shaft did not travel very far but the head disappeared into a bush in the distance. Nobody said anything as Radar stormed off down the fairway, but I marked the spot visually in hopes that I would find a way to retrieve the club later.

When we had finished the round, I brought Phum to the caddie master (who spoke perfect English) and asked him to explain to her that if she managed to recover the club it might be worth quite a bit of money. She let me know through our interpreter that she would not go into the swamp because it was far too dangerous. I persisted and asked the caddie master to help us to get the club back. He recruited a pair of young porters from the clubhouse and we all got into carts and went out to the spot where Riley had thrown away his driver. The caddie master told the young fellows to walk in front of Phum with bamboo sticks in their hands and to make as much noise as they could to frighten off any snakes. Thanks to Phum's keen eye, she found the club in no time.

She then handed it to me with a look that said, "Now what?" I took it to the players' mobile repair truck, which is on site at every tour event, and had the club reshafted as good as new in about five minutes flat. Then I went into the clubhouse and offered it back to Radar "for a finder's fee." When he declined the offer, I sold the club there and then to an amateur who had played in the pro-am for $150 (U.S.). I then went back outside and tipped the caddie master and boy porters $10 each. The rest of the money went to Phum, and you can imagine how happy this made her. When the caddie master saw me give her the cash, he said that she would be robbed on the way home and that I should give the money to him. "I will mind it for her," he said.

I did not fancy that. "I have a better idea," I said.

I asked one of the courtesy car drivers if he would take Phum home and he kindly agreed. We then filled the car with half a dozen of the girl caddies. Squeezed together in the back seat, the girls giggled constantly at the unprecedented treat of being driven home by car. Phum lived less than a mile away but that did not take away from the feeling of enjoyment and adventure. When her parents saw the car outside their little wooden house, they rushed out and gave the driver and me a huge welcome. We were taken inside for tea and fruit—a big honour. But then, $120 was probably the equivalent of a month's wages or more to Phum's family. It

The one and only Tiger Woods.

was no wonder that they were "over the moon" about it.

On the golf course the next day, Padraig and I were quite surprised when we spotted Phum's mother holding a lovely bowl of fruit that she had for the two of us. And for the rest of the week, at the exact, same spot on the course, this enjoyable and very welcome "fruit stop" was repeated.

At one point during the week, I learned that the Thai girls loved to eat ice cream. After mentioning this to Billy Foster, Darren Clarke's caddie, he and I decided that we would give them a little treat when the tournament was over. At the appropriate time, we had a big box of ice cream delivered to the caddie shack. There must have been a hundred girls altogether and we treated them all for less than 20 quid. I am sure that Billy and I were the first senior male caddies ever to sit inside that caddie shack. The girls put on a little singsong for us, and even though we did not understand a single word, it was great fun and certainly one of the highlights of a most enjoyable trip.

I really would like to go back to Thailand sometime. It is

such a lovely place and the Thai people are fantastic. Life is hard there, but Thais seem to smile their way through it.

By the way, that '98 Johnny Walker Classic in Thailand was the first time I began to appreciate how good a player Tiger Woods was becoming. Going into the final nine holes, Tiger was well behind what I thought was an unbeatable Ernie Els. But Tiger hunted him down and eventually won a very exciting play-off with some stunning golf. The Thai people went wild. Since his mother is from there, they consider Tiger one of their own.

Dubai

In my opinion, the Emirates Golf Club in Dubai, Saudi Arabia is the eighth wonder of the world. It is one of the fastest growing cities on the globe and golf is very much a part of the developing tourist attractions there. The two beautiful courses that are used for the Dubai Classic are built in the desert and are quite remarkable in many ways, not the least in the manner in which they were constructed. They are also tremendous tests of golfing skills and I can only imagine how much it must have cost to build such lush layouts in the middle of the desert.

The first step in construction was to pump water from a man-made canal nearby to create four artificial lakes. The lakes are used as hazards for the golfers, and they provide the basis of the irrigation system essential to keep the grass green and healthy. As often happens on new golf courses, the lakes eventually became a habitat for wildlife and in a most pleasant way added to the interest of the surroundings. Less than 50 years ago, Dubai was basically a camel hitching post

I was gasping for a cup of tea in Dubai, but the trophy was considered out-of- bounds!

in the desert. Now it is a bustling metropolis with every modern facility, and a throbbing nightlife. Visitors can enjoy the luxury of some of the best value, high-quality shopping anywhere on earth.

I used to really look forward to the special enjoyment of Dubai's night-time horse racing under floodlights. The atmosphere engendered is quite unique. The best horses and all the top class European jockeys perform there regularly, and it is the home of one of the most successful racing stables ever: Sheikh Mohammed's Gandolphen group. One thing that is unusual about horse racing in Dubai is that there are no on-course bookmakers. Therefore, there isn't any betting. It's mainly a social night out for the locals. Everyone puts on their best robes, they bring their picnic supplies, and they socialise. The Arabs can promenade as well as the French and Italians any day. Many go there to people-watch as much as they go for the horse races.

Sheikh Mohammed's private clubhouse and dressing rooms at Royal Emirates Golf Club in Dubai, Saudi Arabia.

I was lucky to meet George McGrath, a famous jockey from Ireland, who was working as a trainer for Sheikh Mohammed. George wised me up about many things including taking me to the British Club nearby where I was able to place a bet because the club members ran their own "book" out of the sight of the Arabs. It was harmless, but it meant one could have an interest in the traditional manner. George also tipped me off about a horse that was owned by Sheikh Mohammed named Lamtarra. I had a successful wager on him that very evening and a much more lucrative one later that same year when the horse won the Epsom Derby.

Sheikh Mohammed has his own clubhouse on a hill over-looking the Emirates courses. It is an exact replica of the real clubhouse, and it is an amazing structure both inside and outside. It's designed to look like a bedouin's tent, and I have never seen anything as spectacular in all my travels. Inside the clubhouse, the furnishings and fittings must have cost millions. You are actually afraid to go to the toilet because everything is so shiny, golden, and plush. The Sheikh is rarely seen. If he is on the golf course, he is constantly surrounded by about 40 bodyguards. Nobody who isn't allowed can get near the guy. Watching all these people walking down the fairway in a group was like being in Thailand all over again.

In 1989, my employer, Des Smyth, and two other Irish players were in contention to win the tournament on the last day. Des, David Feherty, and Eamon Darcy fought it out with Seve Ballesteros down the finishing straight. Darcy won, so we all made it our business to be there for the prize presentation. I was mooching around, looking for somebody to talk to, when I suddenly realised that the Sheikh himself was standing right beside me. As I always do when an opportunity arises, I struck up a conversation. I loosened him up by saying what an impressive horse Lamtarra was, and that I had seen him leaving the opposition standing the previous night. I told the Sheikh that I had seen him at the Irish Derby at the Curragh the previous year and that I might see him there again later that year because I always tried to go to that event and always took a particularly keen interest in his horses. He was delighted and seemed to be as down-to-earth a guy as you could imagine. He chatted away quite happily without any sign of the security people that usually surround him. My relaxed attitude toward royalty was paying off once more. Treat them like normal people and they will respond in kind. Before leaving him in peace, I told him a little story that I think he enjoyed:

There was this thirsty Arab walking through the desert looking for an oasis, when he saw signs of life way off in the distance. It was not on his direct path but he took a detour hoping that he would find water. But his hopes were dashed because all he found was a little old man sitting at a small table, selling neckties.

"Please, I am dying of thirst, can you give me some water?"

"I do not have any water," the old man said, "but will you

buy a necktie?"

"I do not want a necktie. I want water!"

"Okay, okay", the old man said. "I cannot force you to do so even though I really think you should. But to show you what a fair and reasonable man I am, I will tell you that if you go over that hill, and travel about four miles beyond it, there is a nice restaurant. I am sure you will get all the water you could want there."

The Arab thanked him and jogged over the hill and into the distance. Three hours later the little old man was gathering up his ties, putting them into a suitcase, getting ready to leave when back over the hill, this time crawling on all fours, came the thirsty Arab.

"Could you not find the restaurant?" the old man asked.

"I found it all right," the Arab gasped, "but they wouldn't serve me without a necktie!"

South Africa

When the World Cup was played in Cape Town in 1996, it allowed me to make my first trip to South Africa. I was met at the golf club by a big African caddie named Jumbo who had recently joined the European Tour but had returned home for this particular event to caddie for his fellow countryman, Clinton Whitelaw. Even though I didn't know Jumbo well, he introduced me to the locals as "Irish Johnny, the boss man of the European Caddies." How he came up with that is anybody's guess. Perhaps seniority means more in African society than it does at home, where there is not always the respect for age that there should be. Jumbo was actually back on his home patch where he was a well-known and highly respected figure at the Houghton Country Club. After that flattering and exaggerated introduction by Jumbo, the local caddies granted me a status that I have not often enjoyed elsewhere. Jumbo was a pretty apt name for my new friend because he was absolutely enormous, six-foot-four and 280 pounds in his socks.

Jumbo and his African caddie friend, Justice, at Spawell Golf Center in Dublin. Enjoying their company are my children and my sister, Nancy Slevin.

Jumbo had grown up in nearby Soweto so he took me under his wing and showed me parts of Johannesburg and Cape Town that very few of its own white residents (let alone visitors) had seen. I saw the good, the bad, and the ugly sights of the area. When I told Jumbo that the very idea of apartheid made me sick, he smiled and said that we were "brothers."

"Back in Ireland we do not have many coloured people but we still have class discrimination," I said. "Discrimination is discrimination, and it manifests itself in man's inhumanity to his fellow man everywhere you go in the world. It happens to be more easy to identify in Africa, that's all."

It turned out to be a highly enjoyable and educational

week for me. Thanks to Jumbo, I learned at least one valuable lesson in South Africa: all that anyone needs to be happy is to have good health and hope. The health part applies to everyone, everywhere you go, but the hope of a better life and the freedom to achieve it is only a recent phenomenon in Cape Town. The rich, white African people that I observed struck me as being uptight, defensive, psychologically miserable and deficient in morale because they were so concerned about their futures since the apartheid regime ended. All the money and luxuries in the world were of no use to them in such circumstances because they were clearly fearful that it all might be taken away from them at any moment.

When I mentioned a piece of my father's homespun philosophy to Jumbo, that "Happiness is a state of mind, and that it is better to be on the bottom going up than on the top going down," his eyes lit up and he smiled broadly. He gave me an approving thump on the back with his huge fist, which knocked the stuffing out of me. "You right, man," he chortled, "you right!"

I have been all over the world and seen many varied and wonderful sights. But I have never been stopped in my tracks to such an extent and felt the need to use the term "breathtaking" about scenery as often as I was in South Africa. It is a fantastic country. The incredible vastness of the deep blue sky overawed me. The bright sun, the vivid red clay, the purple mountains and the pearly white clouds could not have been more different from the greens and greys of Ireland.

On the other hand, South Africa was dangerous if you did not know your way around. It was dangerous in the bush (wild animals) and dangerous in the city (muggers). But with Jumbo by my side, I felt safe. He was so big and strong, I was sure that not even a lion would dare to tackle him.

The living conditions in the shantytowns stunned me. I could not believe that so many people could live in such close proximity to each other. The tin and timber huts that passed for homes would be only considered fit for farmyard animals in Ireland. Toilet facilities and running water were minimal and primitive. In spite of these hardships, I sensed a tremendous feeling of optimism in the people. They may have had practically nothing in the way of worldly goods—apart from state-of-the-art radios and televisions—but they had heart and vigour in abundance. Music seemed to be everywhere, and it was a happy, throbbing music that made you want to dance and sing all day long. My buddy, Jumbo, was keen to show me as much as could possibly be fit in between our chores at the country club. However, he also warned me not to go anywhere without his protection.

"I'll be your minder, Irish John," he kept saying over and over. "I'll look after you."

I am not easily frightened or prone to being nervous but I had no intention of leaving my protector's side, especially in Johannesburg, which was the most intimidating and threatening environment I'd ever experienced. Every night we went down into the bowels of shantytown for a couple of drinks. One time, Jumbo took me to a pub that was cobbled together out of the standard, haphazard mixture of timber and tin. There was little ventilation and no air conditioning, so you can imagine how warm and stuffy it became when the place got crowded. The pub was called "The Hole in the Wall." I might very well have been the first white person ever to set foot in it. I enjoyed the local brew, which was a darn sight better than any dishwater English beer that I've tasted in the past. Jumbo, who did not like beer and drank a nonalcoholic diluted orange drink instead, stood beside me at all times, telling me periodically not to worry, he was there to look after me. Even when I needed to go to the toilet, Jumbo came with me. Knowing that I was constantly under the studied gaze of the locals made me slightly uneasy at first. I finally decided that I needed to find a way to make them relax and accept my presence. Eventually, the impromptu karaoke session that seemed to evolve every night provided me with my big opportunity when somebody suggested that

"White John" sing a song. Pretending not to be nervous, I **137**
stood up in front of the crowd of customers.

"I want to dedicate my song to Nelson Mandela!" I said.
And with that, the whole place erupted in cheering and clap-ping. I then proceeded to give them my own rousing Dublin *South Africa*
version of *My Way*. After that piece of inspired thinking, I
won the hearts and minds of the customers of "The Hole in
the Wall" and I was able to relax. Everyone called me "White
Johnny," and for the rest of the week neither Jumbo nor I
had to put our hands in our pockets to buy another drink.

When we were in the "Hole" one evening, Jumbo told me
a little bit about his life history. He was a proud member of
the Zulu tribe and his real name was Fana Joseph Mthembu.
In some ways his story is similar to my own. At the age of 12
he began caddying at the exclusive Houghton Country Club
in Johannesburg in order to earn some badly needed money
to help his mother feed her large family. He told me that ever
since he first became involved in golf, he has loved it passionately. He even took his love for the game further than I did:
as a youngster he helped to build a makeshift course near his
parents' hut in Soweto. Tin cans were buried in the hard and
dusty ground and a carefully crafted golf club made from an
abandoned metal pipe was shared by all and sundry. During
warm evenings there was great excitement as Jumbo and his
friends shared the only homemade club between them and
made up games with small side bets. To tell you the truth, it
sounded strikingly similar to the antics that took place
among the caddies at the Castle Golf Club in Dublin. But little did we know that by comparison, we were nearly million-
aires compared with what was going on in Soweto. Just as I
did, Jumbo worked his way up through the pecking order to
become a fully-fledged professional caddie, working first on
the South African circuit and eventually the European Tour.

******

For the World Cup event, members of the golf club generously housed all the visiting European caddies. Five of us
stayed in a great big fortress overlooking the course. Within
easy walking distance of the clubhouse, high walls and security
gates surrounded it and there were giant floodlights all over
the property. Two savage rottweilers roamed the gardens at
night with an air of menace. On our first night, our host insisted
on taking us all downtown for a fabulous meal in a magnificent restaurant. We had been well-warned not to stray off on
our own, but Paul Lawrie's caddie, Gary, was young, foolish,
and headstrong and much too curious for his own good about
any possible nightspots that might be in the area. He did a
disappearing act after dinner. Our host, who had nearly spoiled
the fabulous meal for me by spending the whole evening criticising the black Africans, was not at all pleased by Gary's
action. He refused to allow us to go look for him, so we eventually went home without him. At around midnight, I was
awakened by a terrible commotion in the garden. I looked out
my window and saw a nearly naked Gary sitting on top of one
of the gate pillars, sobbing, while the two rottweilers sat below,
waiting patiently for him to drop into their jaws once more.
When the owner of the house rescued him, Gary was in a
pitiful state. He had been mugged, robbed, stripped, and
attacked by more than mere dogs. All of his money, his watch
and ring had been taken. The next morning, insult was heaped
upon injury when Gary was asked to leave his magnificent
free lodgings because he had not obeyed the house rules. I
could not bear the way our host had spoken about his black
neighbours the night before and I politely declined to go out
to dinner with him again, but I did not have sufficient princi-
ples to leave my magnificent sleeping quarters or say anything inflammatory. I also made sure that for the rest of the
week that I was escorted back from "the Hole" by Jumbo and
safely indoors before those dogs were let loose.

Meanwhile, back at the Country Club, I could not believe the treatment that was being handed out to the local black caddies. I have never seen anything so barbaric. It was worse than anything I could ever have imagined. The local black caddies were treated worse than animals in a zoo! The caddie master seemed to fancy himself as the ringmaster in a circus because all day long he strode around, swishing a long and springy bamboo-like stick, barking out orders. I never saw him use it, mind you, but he sure looked as if he would have enjoyed the opportunity. The home caddies were all corralled and locked up in a steel cage, which was located in the machinery compound about a quarter of a mile from the clubhouse. When I saw the situation I could not believe my eyes. It reminded me of a scene from a prisoner-of-war movie. I was told to be wary because many of the caged caddies liked to chew a leaf called "chat." It gave them a "high" and it made them act aggressively. During the day, the caddies were only allowed out of the cage if they had been chosen to go onto the golf course by a member and were paid between £2 and £3 per round, a fraction of what us Europeans and Jumbo earned. Now their meagre livelihoods were being interfered with by the arrival of professional caddies from elsewhere and they did not like one bit of it. Jumbo told me that if any of those fellows saw one of us going out with one of their "regular" bags, they would be capable of sticking a knife in him. When I heard that I was very glad that Padraig Harrington was not a member. What was truly amazing was the way that Jumbo accepted the situation. I could never have done that. I would never have been able to take that treatment so seemingly casually. When I started mouthing off about it, he told me that I should mind my own business because it was not my problem. (Before departing at the end of the week, Jumbo and I organised as many players and caddies as we could to give us their unwanted shoes and clothes and we went down to the cage and handed them out. That left a nice thought behind and brought some happiness to a pretty grim situation.)

On the final day of the tournament, I was on the practise ground with Harrington when who should walk up to me but "The Big Easy," Ernie Els (who, I found out, is called Theodore at home).

"Reilly, I heard you were you in 'The Hole' the other night."

"I was there the last *three* nights," says I, proud as punch.

"I would not go within a hundred miles of that place," Enie said. "It is the most dangerous pub in all of Africa."

I said, "Ernie, you wouldn't go there because of your Afrikaans accent. Thanks to my *Dublin* accent, I am now an honorary member of 'The Hole.' Besides, I was always safe as houses there because I had Jumbo to mind me!"

I hardly need to tell you that "Theodore" was completely flabbergasted by that piece of information and went away shaking his head in disbelief.

******

During the tournament, I had been delighted to see my great friend from Adare, the pub owner Pat Collins, in our gallery. He was on one of his exotic vacations he takes from time to time. After the round, with Jumbo as our guide, Pat and I went sightseeing. We drove up the side of Table Mountain and also went to see Nelson Mandela's prison cell on Robben Island. How that man survived his long ordeal there is truly astonishing.

Exactly one year after my visit to South Africa I had the chance to repay Jumbo's wonderful hospitality when he came to Dublin for the European Open at the K-Club. I invited him to stay in my home in Tallaght. I told Margaret and the children that we were going to have a visitor, but I did not elaborate. Margaret pointed out that we had no spare bedroom—with six children, how could we?

"I am sorry," she said, "but your friend will have to sleep on the couch."

"No problem," I replied. Remembering the conditions in Soweto, I was sure that sleeping on our couch would be a comparative luxury. Margaret dutifully tidied up the house, got out her best cutlery and tablecloth in honour of our guest, and began to cook dinner while I drove over to the K-Club to collect Jumbo.

He was delighted to see me. When we got to my house, I told him to hop out of the car and to wait a few minutes until I had parked and gone inside. I wanted to be able to see the excitement that Jumbo would cause when he came through the door. Our youngest, Noel, was six years old at the time and a fearless little bundle of energy. He was so tiny we called him "Half-pint." When we heard a knock on the door, I told Half-pint to answer it. Seeing Jumbo standing at our doorstep, Noel fled in terror. "Mammy, Mammy," he shrieked, "there is a big monster at the door!"

It was so funny. I never saw anyone move so fast in my life. Jumbo laughed heartily, quite used to receiving the same reaction at home in Africa. I invited him inside. After the initial shock wore off, my kids settled down and made my African minder very welcome. The kids loved Jumbo and were as proud as could be when he took them down to a local shop to buy them sweets. They introduced Jumbo to all of their pals who followed him around like he was the Pied Piper. He was so big everyone was in awe of him. He became an instant celebrity. He was extremely gentle and kind to the local kids and they still talk about his deep-throated "Paul Robeson" laugh. It was a great week and the kids never left the man alone for a moment. When Jumbo was leaving, he invited us all back to Soweto to stay with him. It was kind of him, but I doubt that it will ever happen.

Two "Bosses" and a "gopher." Left to right: Ben Dunne, former Taoiseach Charles J. Haughey, and myself at Kinsealy, Mr. Haughey's home.

"The Boss"

A man who has had probably the biggest influence on my life because he is such a larger than life character is the warm-hearted and generous (but a bit eccentric) Ben Dunne. Some people call him "The Big Fella" but I have always called him "The Boss." Even though he has been hugely successful in his business career, he still saw himself as a champion of the underdog. And I am only one of many who have had good reason to be thankful for his generosity. All that I have ever been able to give him in return is some dubious, if well-intentioned, golf advice. Ben is a paradox; he often reaches out to help those with troubles, (many young Irish golf professionals, for example, have been sponsored by Ben before they got on their feet and were able to support themselves), but in business he's known for being completely ruthless. I have often sat impatiently in his large office on St. Stephen's Lane waiting for him to finish wheeling and dealing so that we could head out to Portmarnock for a golf date.

While driving hard bargains was Ben's stock-in-trade, he

was never like that with me. I swear that I have witnessed him carrying on five or six different telephone conversations with suppliers from all over the world and all at the same time. Figures would be flying in all denominations and directions. Deals worth hundreds of thousands of pounds were being transacted on what appeared to be an impulse. I have always said that if Ben Dunne had been the Prime Minister of Ireland during the bad times of the 1980s, we would have enjoyed the Celtic Tiger boom years a lot sooner.

The Boss is not a bad golfer either. He plays off a single figure handicap, is very competitive, and he likes to gamble on the golf course as much as he does in business — especially if there are a few pros in the game. Des Smyth is a great friend and regular playing partner of The Boss and they are a tough combination when there is a large stake on the line. In particular, Ben loves to see opponents sweating over a sum that is peanuts to him but not to them.

I have also been on a number of overseas golf trips with Ben and his friends. I never went as a caddie, though. It was strictly holiday time for me. Plus, the guys always used buggies because of the warm temperatures. I usually ended up being the activities organiser, chauffeur, gopher, and general dog's body. My number one task was making sure everybody got to the first tee on time after the previous night's revelries.

On one such trip we stayed at Innisbrook, a fabulous 63-hole golf resort near Tampa, Florida. Smythie was with us and he decided that he would hop over to Orlando for a practise round because he had been invited to compete in Arnold Palmer's Bay Hill Invitational the following March. The Boss asked me to make the necessary arrangements, but doing so turned into a bit of a saga.

Now I admit that I must have looked a bit of a sight when I approached the desk clerk to ask him to find me a rental car. I was wearing a scruffy tee shirt, baggy shorts, no socks, trainers, and a floppy hat.

"I want to hire a car for a trip to Orlando tomorrow, please."

The clerk looked me over and I could tell that his mind was working along the lines of : *Uh-oh, what have we got here?*

"Sorry, sir," he said, "but we don't have any cars available at the moment. Would a van be sufficient?"

"No, I would like a car. A limousine with a driver, preferably."

"Do you know how much that will cost?" he asked.

"No, but it does not matter because Mr. Ben Dunne will be taking care of it." This obviously meant nothing to him. He hemmed and hawed and then told me that it would take several days to find a limousine and that I should have booked it a week in advance. I thought this was ridiculous, so I asked the fellow if he would be kind enough to get John Huston on the phone.

I knew John well. He was not the touring professional but the very efficient and courteous General Manager of the Innisbrook Resort. He saw to it that our little group of big-spending Irishmen received first-class attention and service at all times. He knew the score and often joined us for a chat and a joke. Some members of our group spent more money at his resort *in one day* than many of his regular customers would probably spend in a month.

"John, I am having a bit of problem," I told the GM. "Your clerk says he cannot get me a limousine so that Smythie can go to Bay Hill tomorrow."

I then handed the phone to the clerk so that he could listen to "some thunder" from John. About two minutes later, pouring sweat and sporting a loosened necktie, the guy said, "Mr. O'Reilly, you may pick up the limousine at 10 o'clock tomorrow at the car rental depot in Palm Harbor."

"No way." says I. "I want it here at the resort at 10 a.m. and with driver attached."

"Impossible, sir," he said. "It cannot be done." This led to another phone call to Huston and a similar result as the first.

"Mr. O'Reilly," the clerk said after listening to John again, "your limousine will be here at reception at 10 a.m. sharp. Have a nice day."

"Thank you," I said sweetly.

When I saw Smythie about 15 minutes later I told him everything had been arranged. He then proceeded to put the tin hat on it by saying that somebody had just told him that it would take two and a half hours to drive to Bay Hill. If traffic was heavy, it could take up to four hours.

"Much too much driving in this heat," he said. "Cancel the car. We're staying put."

You could have knocked me down with a feather! And all I could think about was that I had to go back and face that clerk. Before I had to, however, Ben Dunne arrived on the scene. Des told him he wasn't going to Bay Hill because it would take too long.

"Well then, Smythie," The Boss says, "I think you should *fly* over to Bay Hill. Reilly, hire a helicopter."

Now I had done many weird and wonderful things in my life up to then, but hiring helicopters was not one of them. So, back down to the desk I go where calmness had only recently been restored.

"Cancel that limousine, please" says I. The clerk's reaction was almost explosive.

"Do you know how much trouble you put me through to get it?" he says. "This is just too much!"

"Hold your horses a minute," I said. "I want to hire a helicopter instead." Well, you could have heard a pin drop when I said that. Everybody in the office stopped what they were doing and looked at me.

"A helicopter?" the clerk said in disbelief. "Do you know how much that will cost?"

"I do not care what it costs" I replied. I placed Ben Dunne's platinum credit card on his desk. "This card could buy for the whole resort."

He continued to stare at me for a few moments. "I'm sure," he said finally, "that you will have to go to Clearwater Airport to meet the helicopter."

"Like hell we will, Mate. Call Mr. Huston again." The clerk

Arnold Palmer and the author at Bay Hill Golf Club in Orlando, Florida in 1996. We renewed an acquaintance that went back to 1975 when our "accommodations" at a tournament in Berlin were a U.S. Army billet.

does so, explains the situation, listens, then hangs up.

"Mr. O'Reilly," says he, "your helicopter will be right beside the putting green at 10 a.m. tomorrow morning."

"Thank you," I said with a nod and a grin.

The next day everything went as smooth as silk. Ben came with us to Bay Hill and we met Arnold Palmer, who was playing ahead of us with a group of friends. Afterward, we went into the Spike Bar. Arnold was in the middle of a huddle trying to figure out who owed who what and how much. It was just like any other fourball anywhere in the world.

On another trip to Innisbrook, it was decided at the last minute that I should be allowed to play in the "golf tournament" that had been organised. It had been years and years since I had played a competitive round of golf. I borrowed John Huston's clubs and gladly accepted the handicap of 18 that was give to me. One of the lads, meat baron Peter Henshaw, always ran a book on the tournament and he quoted me as the complete outsider at 40/1 odds. Actually, I thought that was rather generous so I put a few quid on myself. So did a few of the others, including Smythie and The Boss. Thanks to a hot putter (12 one-putts) I managed to score very well. Coming down the difficult last hole I knew I needed a par 4 to tie with odds-on favourite John Mulholland (once the mayor of Galway), who was already in the clubhouse with a score of 42 points (6 under par). I put my second shot into a green-side bunker but I was quite close to the hole and short bunker shots like that had never been any trouble for me. I got it up and down without too much distress.

Play-off!

There was a fierce rush of excitement as guys hurried to place their bets with Henshaw on the outcome of the shootout. After everybody settled down, we gathered once more at the first tee. There were about a dozen carts in all and the buzz of excitement was palpable. I was used to that, of course, but it was slightly different being the *player* and not the *caddie*. Johnny McGonigle ("The Gunner" as we called him) volunteered to be my buggy driver and adviser. Henshaw approached me and asked me if I wanted to hedge my bets.

"What do you mean?" I asked.

"If you sell me half your stake. That way, you are certain to come out ahead."

"No way!" says I. "That would only reduce my winnings."

I knew I could not outplay Mullers, but I was confident that I could *out think* him. Besides, I was having too much fun. I was already ahead in my own mind and it was only a few dollars. I well knew that there was no point in playing if I did not believe that I could win. But then my so-called "adviser" decided to express his opinion.

"Johnny," The Gunner said, "you would be wise to accept Peter's offer. There is a lot of moolah involved."

But I would not budge. So the lads began placing even more bets before getting into their buggies to wait for the play-off.

After I won the coin toss to hit first, I whacked this horrible yoke into the trees on the right. Mulholland hit a boomer 250 yards down the middle. Gunner and I rode down to my ball and studied my predicament with great care. Noticing Smythie watching me from the fairway, I thought to myself, *What would he do if he was in this situation?*

Finally, I said to Gunner, "Hand me the 5-wood. I see a shot."

"Are you mad?" he replied. "Who do you think you are, Des Smyth?"

"Just give me the [bleeping] club." Miraculously, I hit this low cutter which took advantage of the undulations on the fairway and the ball hopped, skipped, and jumped its way up to the edge of the green. Mulholland was stunned, but he managed to find the green safely with his much shorter approach shot. We both putted up dead and halved the hole. The next hole was a short, reachable par 5 with water in front of the green. I hit another low cutter but it was grand (for me) and in the fairway. Mayor John hit another superb tee shot 40 yards past mine.

This time I decided to play smart. "Give me the wedge, Gunner. I am going to lay up."

"You can't do that!" he said excitedly. "Mullers will reach the green easily from where he is. You have to go for the green and try to match him. C'mon, Johnny, do not concede the advantage and hand it to him on a plate."

"Gunner, I have seen all of this before. He doesn't have a gimme four so I'm going to play the percentages. I'm going for my par and I'm going to let *him* make the mistakes."

The Gunner was jumping up and down with apoplexy but I ignored him and went ahead and knuckled an iron shot into position, nicely short of the water. Now it was Mulholland's turn. This was long before the movie, *Tin Cup*, but a replica of its famous final scene was what was about to transpire, and all the wisdom that I had picked up from caddying over the years was about to pay off big-time. Reaching the green was possible for the mayor all right, but only if he managed to hit his best shot. And it was a big "if" under the circumstances, with all of that money riding on the outcome. He was too proud to give up the advantage he'd gained by hitting such a fine tee-shot and he erroneously felt "obliged" to go for it.

After doing his deep breathing exercises "Mullers" let fly with a fairway wood. It was a good shot and it soared over the water, but ... it landed on the slope of the bank in front of the green and slid slowly backward into the agua. He immediately reloaded and did exactly the same thing, making the classic amateur mistake of not moving forward to the water's edge and then hitting his fourth shot from there.

Mulholland went for it a third time, finding the green at last. I now faced my own shot over the water. I was suddenly nervous because now I had something to lose, so I made sure to keep my eye on the ball and swing hard. My wedge shot flew safely over the water, landed on a slope 12 feet beyond the hole and spun back four feet short of the cup.

I could not believe that I had won! Fistfuls of dollars were plunged into my hands and Peter Henshaw was cleaned out, but not irrevocably, I was sure.

We all marched into the men's grillroom for a rowdy presentation of the Ben Dunne plaque. This was followed by a few magnums of champagne, French fries, fried chicken, buffalo wings or whatever took our fancy. An unwritten rule of the competition was that the winner must pick up the tab for the evening's food and drink. But when I went to pay, I was told that all the fellows who had backed me had clubbed together and paid for everything out of their winnings. I was allowed to keep my little windfall. Although he would not admit it, I am certain that Ben Dunne was the instigator of that idea.

As I said earlier, The Boss has always been champion of the underdog.

Nanny and Gopher

"Johnny," Waltz says to me, "I want you to make all the calculations and decisions—just hand me a club."

The one and only time I willingly and completely "took over" a player was at the French Open in Chantilly. Smythie had missed the cut and Philip Walton, who had qualified right on the limit, had fired his caddie. Philip surprised me not only by asking me to go with him for the weekend, but also to make all of the club decisions and read every line on the greens as well. Now, he and I go back a long way and have always been the best of pals, so I was reassured that if I made a mistake he would not hold it against me. It even occurred to me that if I gave him the wrong club, he would probably think that I had done it as a prank. That's how laid-back he is about golf. Waltz is a very easygoing character unlike so many other professional golfers. However, I do not think my nerves could have stood all that responsibility on a regular basis—for Philip or anyone else. In my opinion, it's a recipe for disaster. Any caddie who believes he can influence the way his man (his boss) plays the game is exercising self-delusion, and the relationship is heading for the rocks. The advent of such modern aids as yardage books and markings on the golf course has not made clubbing greatly more easy than the old method of "eyeballing" the green from afar. Any caddie worth his salt *should* eyeball the shot before looking at his yardage book. Nine times out of ten, he will find his natural instinct and senses will be correct.

At Chantilly, for some reason, Waltz wanted to simplify matters. I think he was only being lazy, but when things started to go nicely for us, he allowed himself to relax, go along for the ride and enjoy the experience. If more competitive golf was played in that frame of mind, the scores would be lower. In any case, over the two days I did not get a single decision wrong and Waltz shot back-to-back 65s — probably the best weekend of golf he ever played. In fact, he came from flat last after 36 holes to finish a creditable fourth. It was strictly a one-off arrangement, though, for both of us. I was proud of myself but mighty relieved when the "experiment" was over. I also enjoyed my bonus money, but would not like to have to do it again. At the game's highest level, golf is an exercise in damage limitation. It is all a matter of keeping mistakes to a minimum. Avoiding bogeys is every bit as important as scoring birdies. Touring pros hate to make unforced errors (such as hitting a "perfect" shot with the "wrong" club). If by any chance the man on their bag had made the slightest contribution to such a mistake, it would be exaggerated to disastrous proportions and job security would become an issue. But just as I was proud of my efforts, Waltz was mighty satisfied with himself too. After all, wasn't he the one who hit all the shots? Of course, he didn't even consider asking Smythie to release me. That's a golfer for you: ungrateful to the end. Caddies do not have their little egos massaged very often.

Actually, I have never believed in all that stuff about a caddie needing to advise his player on every shot. You can give the player perfect yardage, give advice about the wind direction, the way the land slopes, how the ball is likely to react when it comes back to earth, so on and so forth. But the player has to hit the ball himself. That part of it is out of your control. It is even more fraught with danger on the green where the speed of a putt is every bit as important as the line. How can anyone know how hard *someone else* is going to hit a putt? That is "feel," and how can you know how somebody else feels? Professional golfers already *know* how to play the game; they do not need somebody telling them what to do every five minutes. Far better to keep out of the way, head for the next tee, and let them get on with their own mistakes. That was my motto. I saw the caddie's role as that of a servant, valet, nanny, and "go-fer" far more than that of an adviser. It was primarily a job of "get me this and get me that." And the most important "get me" was the correct yardage.

Once upon a time every caddie had to do his own measurements, which meant that there might be 50 caddies walking around the golf course with their measuring wheels the evening prior to a tournament. The hosting venues grew tired of that interference and the arrangement developed that one person would do the measuring long before the full circus, as we called ourselves, arrived on the scene. The necessary information was then supplied to us in booklet form for a small fee. All the caddie had to do was make the odd spot-check to make sure that the booklet was accurate and possibly add a few extra pieces of information that his individual player might require for a specific purpose based on his particular strategy and tactical approach to playing the game.

One day Smythie asked me to tell him which direction the wind was blowing. Temporarily forgetting my place in the pecking order of things, I let my impatience show and told him he needed a weather forecaster and meteorologist rather than a caddie. Fortunately, he laughed and said that that was very funny. He saw my point of view but can you imagine giving such a flippant answer to Seve Ballesteros? He would "kill" you with one of those piercing looks of his. Actually, I was being temperamental more than funny (for once), a luxury that is normally denied the caddie corps. But I have to say that some of the convoluted and overanalytical conversations I have heard between players and caddies were simply ridiculous. If a player has to be advised in graphic detail what to do all the time, he should not be playing professional golf in my view. It is only when coming down the last few holes, when the pressure is *really* on, that a caddie's input is needed—but always only as a support and a sounding board. It is a very rare occasion indeed when a situation similar to the Van De Velde "incident" at Carnoustie occurs. That is when a caddie might have to almost threaten violence upon his player to make him do "the right thing."

I have found over the years that if I could answer a question with another question about the consequences of any action being considered, I could focus and sharpen my player's mind and at the same time save myself from being blamed if it all went wrong. However, I made sure the words "I told you so" never passed my lips. That would have been virtual hara-kiri. I regard decision-making to be the player's business; he really should know what to do without having to consult anybody. Being alert to any changing circumstances, maintaining a calm environment, acting as a buffer and setting the scene by keeping a close eye on the leader board are all-important inputs by the caddie. But decisions on how to play a particular shot? No thanks, that is the player's problem. On the course the caddie is there primarily to take care of the equipment, keep it clean and dry, and to watch the ball.

I need hardly stress how important it is to be on time, making sure that your player does not get "ambushed" or delayed between the practise ground and the first tee. You would be surprised how difficult this can be sometimes, especially for the top guys and even for lesser mortals when they are playing near their hometown. The number of times that players misread their tee-off time is quite astonishing.

In my experience one can never check one's tee time too often. If a player is late, you can be sure that the caddie will be blamed for it. Being fully prepared and having everything that the player could possibly need during a round of golf packed up and at the ready is vital.

A bit of psychological cunning goes a long way, too. A good caddie is "streetwise," like a bodyguard. He is able to anticipate "trouble" and institute precautions to dodge it. One of the first attributes that a player looks for in a caddie is an ability to be a soul-mate and confidante. There has to be a trusting relationship, similar to that between man and wife. It is a couple's thing: both have to be able to get along and be able to understand and tolerate each other's foibles. The minute a player finds a reason to dislike or distrust his caddie, the partnership is over. Divorces between caddies and players are often executed on the spot and there isn't any alimony. Sometimes a player can get it into his head that a particular caddie is lucky. That little thought will create huge job security because many of the players are peculiarly susceptible to superstition. Pete Coleman, who has caddied for Bernhard Langer for almost 20 years, is actually nicknamed "Lucky." But Pete's nickname is a sham because it actually has its origins in his legendary inability to beat the bookies! The horses and dogs on which he wagers always have the most heartbreaking of hard-luck stories.

It is also quite amazing how many times a player will win soon after he has made a caddie change. Why this should be so is a mystery, but it happens regularly and it is why I have always accepted a casual bag whenever the opportunity arose. A change is as good as a rest. A bit of caddie swapping in midseason for a short period is a frequently indulged-in practise. It is good for everybody concerned. Win, lose, or draw, I have always been happy to go back to my principal employer, loyal and true to the guy who was paying my wages week in and week out.

When Peter Townsend was surprisingly beaten in the first

round of the Irish Professional Match Play Championship at Ballybunion in 1978, a youthful and not very wealthy Arnold O'Connor approached me about taking his bag for his next match and then "let's see how things go." He said he could not afford to pay me but if we managed to progress through a few rounds he would be able to give me "a percentage." I was okay financially because Townsend had, as usual, paid me the week in advance. Since I had nothing better to do, I agreed to O'Connor's offer.

Amazingly, Arnold mowed 'em down like skittles. One fancied player after another fell to his hot putter. In the final, the momentum was unstoppable and he carried off a huge upset by beating David Jones from Bangor, winning on the seventeenth green. Arnold was absolutely and rightly thrilled. He was crowned the Irish Professional Match Play Champion after a very short time as a pro. We celebrated long and hard that night. The next morning, four of us—the great Jimmy Martin who played Ryder Cup golf, Eamon Darcy, Arnold, and myself—set off for Dublin. Unbelievably, because we made so many pit stops along the way, it took us two and a half days to complete the journey.

When I started, caddying on the European Tour was a precarious existence, monetarily, for the vast majority of us. Only the guys working for the top players could make a comfortable living. To seek some security, I always negotiated a subsistence level weekly wage to be paid in advance. If the player did not perform and missed the cut, I could at least get home or onto the next tour stop. To counterbalance this, I had to agree to receive a lower percentage of the final prize money if my player did well. I am not complaining, mind you, just telling you the secrets of the trade. These days the prize funds are so huge that some naïve caddies are inclined to work the other way around and hope for a larger percentage if his player does well. That is a risky business and some players will not agree to it. I have heard players complaining among themselves about having to give their caddie up to

10% of a sizeable winner's cheque. To many of the players, giving a caddie that amount of money appears to be out of proportion to the work they do. I look at it in terms of a lottery and ask critics to remember the poor times. We should not be begrudged for our occasional windfalls. The caddies workday and workweek are long, and if there is a sizeable trek between venues there may not be any time off from one week to the next.

The salary arrangement between a player and his caddie is always a private matter. It is one of the best-kept secrets in the entire world. Even the caddies do not tell each other the private payment arrangements made with their players. But if a player were to renege on his "gentleman's agreement" with his caddie, that breach of trust would be broadcast far and wide and the PGA would be called in to adjudicate. Normally the player is forced to pay up and is reprimanded.

These days the prize money has improved so much that many of the top caddies work for a set weekly wage, plus expenses, and only receive an end-of-season bonus. A piece of the "pie" if the player has a top five finish is not always part of the agreement, but a share of the winning purse might be negotiated at anything from 5% to 10%. In other words, you might have to survive on "fresh air" for a long time, waiting for a good percentage to come along.

It may appear to the outsider that a caddie's work begins on the first tee on Thursday and ends at the eighteenth green on either Friday or Sunday, depending on whether a player makes the cut. Far from it! There is an awful lot of preparation work. First of all, you have to be on site early on the Tuesday morning of the tournament to collect the player's quota of balls and gloves from his equipment sponsor for the week ahead, then be on hand to go along with him for various "obligatory" visits to the practise ground and, of course, a practise round or two as well. A clubhouse locker has to be found for storage purposes. Items of clothing, especially shoes and rain gear, have to be kept clean and dry at all times. If a player has an early tee-time, say 7 a.m., the caddie would need to be at the club at 5:30 a.m. because players always like to do some loosening up before they play. Pretournament practise is usually fairly gentle but those "après round" practise sessions can easily turn into brutal marathon affairs if the player is off the boil (not swinging well). The work can stretch from dawn until dusk because there isn't a time limit to a caddie's day. You are at the Boss's beck and call.

The caddies of the less successful players have to work every bit as hard, if not harder, than their more successful colleagues and for a lot less pay. Once the tournament ends, it is the caddie's job to pack up the equipment and either take it to the airport or put it in the van that is sometimes provided by the PGA. Some players expect their caddie to take care of the equipment and transport it for them to the next venue, as if carrying it around all week is not enough. Those golf bags are an unbelievable weight when they are filled up with shoes, rain gear, and the like. Try travelling by bus or train with one of those things, plus your own gear!

Besides the celebrations and postmortems, my favourite part of the job was the preparation— minding the bag, keeping the player's shoes and clubs clean, all that sort of thing. Most of the players are particularly fussy about their shoes. They really like having shiny shoes. I found this out in Spain one year when I failed to get a bag for the week. In order to earn a few bob, I set up a stall as a shoeshine boy. I was inundated with business and made a cool £500. I was delighted that I had provided the service and so were the players. Sam Torrance said that I should give up caddying and become the "official shoe shine boy" of the European Tour. I thought about it but did not do it. There is a job opportunity there for somebody if they are inclined, I am telling you.

Anyway, I was particularly good at all of the preparation work because I always did it at my leisure the night before. The next morning before setting off, all I had to do was run through my checklist to confirm that all was in order and in place. Enough balls, gloves, towels, sunscreen, a water bottle, sticking plasters, an extra pair of shoelaces, etc. Seriously, you have no idea how important spare shoelaces are. Is the rain gear dry, nicely folded, and ready for action? Some players are extremely superstitious and fussy. Seve will not tolerate a golf ball in his bag that has the number 3 on it. (I often thought that a good way to rattle Seve while playing in his group would be to use only number 3 golf balls!) Many of the players also carry "good luck charms," like coins and stuff. If you managed to lose them, you would be dead.

Nanny and Gopher

Caddies have to be masters of time and motion. After all, if you had to carry about 60 pounds on your back for up to six miles every day you would also be on the lookout for shortcuts of all kinds. Once when I was caddying for Harrington in America, I learned an exceptional energy saver. During a practise round, the legendary caddie Mike "Fluff" Cowan was in our group. (Fluff was Tiger Woods's first professional caddie, and he is a marvellous character in his own right.) At one point, I made a comment to Fluff about how far our players' divots were flying—30 yards or more on every shot—which, naturally, we had to retrieve and replace.

"That is several extra yards of walking on almost every hole," I said. "Do that every day for a week and it's an awful lot of extra walking."

Fluff proceeded to tell me that the way to solve this problem was to pick up a fresh divot on the practise range and put it in my bib pocket. After the first divot of the round flies, I was to repair it with the one in my bib. On my way up the fairway, I would then pick up the fresh one, put it in my bib and use it when needed. And so on and so on. It was brilliant.

During the tournament itself, we were paired with Faldo and his caddie Fanny Sunnesson. At one stage I heard Faldo say, "Keep an eye on that old Irish geezer, Fanny. He would buy and sell you on how to get around a golf course!" I was pleased to hear this, of course, but I did not tell them that I was in Fluff's debt for the energy-saving advice. Fanny, by the way, is no slouch in the caddie stakes and she is well respected and liked by all the other bagmen. But her colleagues did have a laugh at her expense in Jersey one year.

I always liked to go to the Jersey Open a week early so that I could stay with my friends Jerry and Anne Mynes. Plus, there is a kind of unwritten rule that the first caddie to pitch up on the site of the next tournament automatically gets "the franchise" for measuring the yardage and marking the course. (After the other caddies arrive they will buy copies of this information for a small fee.) Since I was there first, Jerry and I combined forces to measure the course the weekend before the tournament. When Fanny came along on Monday, she decided for some reason to do her own marking and in doing so changed some of the spots that I had put down. What she actually did was dig up my marks and paint her own, which made the information in all my booklets wrong. There was fierce confusion. Eventually a caddie committee went to see John Paramour, the head of Rules for the European Tour. When he decided that Fanny should replace my original marks, both of us were saved from a lynching.

Dave Musgrove is a few years my junior. He caddies for Lee Jantzen these days and is one of the most experienced and wisest bagmen that I ever came across. He has "won" the Open Championship twice, first with Seve Ballesteros at Royal Lytham in 1979 when the Spanish maestro had his famous "car park" win. Dave swears that Seve drove into the car parks on purpose to avoid the high grass. "The car park was a lot wider than the fairway," he says. Dave was with Sandy Lyle when the big Scot had his success at Royal St. George's in 1985. The Lyle and Musgrove team also won the 1988 Masters' title. Then the 1998 U.S. Open was won by Jantzen with Dave once more on the bag at Olympic in San Francisco. The USPGA Championship has managed to escape his grasp so far but if he brings that off, he will have a pretty unique caddie grand slam. Musgrove has defined the caddie's role in the following ultrasimple manner.

(1) Show up.

(2) Shut up.

(3) Stay up.

I have repeatedly said that the influence a caddie has on his player is exaggerated and overdone. I am sure Musgrove would heartily agree. One situation that "disproves" the rule was what happened to Sandy Lyle when Dave ceased working for him. Sandy's star waned as suddenly and as dramatically as any that I have ever seen. He sank like a stone. The magnificent long iron play, which he can still produce at will today, has not stopped the decline either. I firmly believe Sandy's problems were caddie related. His decision to dump Musgrove and put a Swedish lady in charge of his bag—one who, it was reported, massaged his toes—was catastrophic.

By far the hardest task for any caddie is coping with a rainy day. The workload increases dramatically (on *and* off the course); you need as many arms as an octopus, and the players are more cranky than usual. They're more prone to remarks such as, "Is that umbrella for you or for me?"

Whenever a player annoyed me with a remark like that, I responded by holding the umbrella in such a position that the drops coming off the side would go straight down the back of his neck. I would execute a delicious payback by innocently saying, "The rain is really heavy, isn't it?"

The bottom line is that, monetarily speaking, most pros are good to their caddie. Amateurs, on the other hand, can be unpredictable when it comes to paying a man his due. I once caddied for a member of the richest family in the world, a cousin of the Sultan of Brunei. Actually, I spent a whole week with him. Normally, I would have discussed terms first. But because this was the Sultan's cousin, I foolishly thought that I was onto a good thing. Especially when my colleague "Olazabal Dave" Renwick, a man noted for his ability to spot a well-paid loop, came over and said, "You will make a right few quid there, Irish John."

I was delighted but, eventually, sadly deluded. I'm telling

you, I did everything I could for the guy except hit the shaggin' ball. At the end of the week I hung around but there was no sign of being paid. I went looking for him. When I found him, I told him I needed my wages. He referred me to his secretary. The secretary was a right so-and-so and acted as if he knew nothing about anything. After a bit of argy-bargy he offered me £50 per day. I told him that that was no good, that it would not even pay for my digs and that I did have to eat, too. So back I went to the Sultan's cousin to let him know that I was not at all happy with my lot. When I explained that I had only been offered £50 per day, he replied that that was a couple of months' wages in Brunei. I told him sharply I did not live in Brunei and that he was not in Brunei *now*. But I was wasting my time because he was a most unsympathetic character. Later I found out that Billy Foster, who caddied for Seve at one time and works for Darren Clarke these days, was given a Rolex watch after caddying for the *real* Sultan. It was the luck of the draw, I suppose—you win some, you lose some.

I got the wrong Sultan!

More Caddie Yarns

A caddie, Johnny McCrossan (R.I.P.), was a good friend of mine and we often roomed together, I never knew his real name. But many are the times he got me into trouble. Usually, it was because the guy would do almost anything for a few pints of beer, and because he involved me in some schemes in an attempt to make an extra few bob.

One evening a group of caddies were sitting around shooting the breeze when along came Johnny with what he claimed was as a sack full of Dunlop "65" golf balls.

"Where did you get them, Johnny?" someone asked. "Did they fall off a lorry?"

"Ah, come on fellas, you are always so suspicious," Johnny replied with a smile. "I got them in the market. What are you offering me? You can make a handy few bob with this lot," he assured us.

One of the caddies put his hand into the sack and pulled out one of the beautifully wrapped balls. "This isn't even a golf ball. It's chocolate shaped to look like a golf ball!"

Poor Johnny had been rumbled. And since none of us had fallen for the trick, we gorged ourselves for the next couple of days on chocolate golf balls. Nobody ever did find out where Johnny got them in the first place, nor did he reveal the source.

Johnny once caddied for Carl Mason in the Greater Manchester Open. At the end of the tournament the early finishers were hanging around, half watching the leaders coming up No. 18. The players were on an upstairs veranda; the caddies were gathered below on the patio. The drinks flowed both upstairs and downstairs and the banter was in full swing. Most of the pros do not mind if his caddie helps himself to a few used gloves, caps, and golf balls at the end of the week. But Johnny continually abused this leniency and literally cleaned out his player's bag at the end of every tournament. Unbeknown to him on that fateful day in Manchester, Johnny was being watched from on high as he removed everything that he possibly could from Carl Mason's golf bag. Not long later, gagging for a pint, he wandered up to Carl. "Any chance of being paid, Boss. I want to get out of here."

"Sure, Johnny, no problem." Mason then proceeded to leave him short on the amount.

"That's not right, Boss," Johnny said. "You've left me short a couple of quid."

Carl just smiled. "Well, I'm sure you will get more than that for all of the stuff you nicked out my bag."

That was the end of the matter and it was a good lesson for all of the other caddies, too.

******

The first time Titleist gave the European Tour a supply of brand-new balls for the players to use when practicing at tournaments, a guy like Johnny McCrossan could not resist the temptation. The range at Wentworth is a bit on the short side, so the players were hitting their drivers into the trees

and bushes at the end of it. Johnny organised a few of the
lads to go down to the end of the fairway with some refuse
sacks. They gathered golf balls by the hundreds, all of which
were sparkling new, having been struck only once. Johnny
thought he was in a "finder's keepers" paradise and that he
was going to earn a month's wages in a single afternoon. But
the Wentworth professional at the time was Bernard
Gallacher, a dour and canny Scot. Nobody would cod him
too easily. He sat there like a jungle cat, waiting patiently and
silently. He did not move a muscle until the boys were laden
down with their golf ball booty. Then and only then did he
pounce and relieve them of their heavy loads.

******

Of all the schemes and rackets I have been involved in, by
far the most financially successful was during the Open
Championship a few years ago at Muirfield in Scotland.
Smythie had failed to make it through the qualifying rounds
and he decided to go home to practise for the Dutch Open
the following week. I decided to hang around just in case one
of the exempt players from overseas might need a caddie.
With Holland coming up the next week, it was cheaper for
me to stay put. Besides, there was always a bit of action on
the fringes of the Open Championship and I did not want to
miss any of it.

As it turned out, I did not get a bag and one of my best
caddie buddies, "Camlough George," fared likewise. The sig-
nificance of that strange nickname had to do with the village
in Scotland from where George originated and the fact that
there were two other Georges on Tour: "Turnberry George"
and "Comeback George." It may seem unusual but very rarely
did I ever find out the real names of many of my colleagues
among the caddie fraternity, or the true source of their nick-
names in many cases. That information was "classified" and

considered private and you would be told to "mind your own business" if you asked. At Muirfield, Camlough and I were hanging around doing little and running out of money fast. With no income for that week assured, we had to find a good scheme that would bring in some cash.

What we did was go to the R&A office and buy two tickets at a special discount. Then we went down to one of the large car parks and waited for a busload of Camlough's parsimonious fellow countrymen to arrive. We were certain that no true Scot would be able to resist the lure of a genuine bargain. When our first load of prospective customers arrived, we approached them and asked if they would like to buy two daily tickets for less than the price of one.

The usual reply was, "What's the catch?"

The catch was indeed exactly that, a catch. George had found a tennis ball and had cut a slit in it with a penknife. "We will sell you a pair of tickets at half price," we told the interested Scots, "on the condition that once you get inside you will put the tickets into the tennis ball and throw it back over the hedge."

It worked like a dream. We did a roaring trade and the R&A Office was blissfully unaware of our "enterprise," which was costing them a fortune. We took turns acting as lookout and our little scheme was never spotted. I must confess that it felt good to get one over the stuffed shirts of the R&A, and Secretary Keith Mackenzie in particular. How I disliked him! We made a small fortune and lived like kings in Holland the following week.

******

The American John Jacobs was a well-known "wild man" on the world tours of golf before he finally mellowed in "old age" when he joined the lucrative seniors' circuit in the U.S. "Big Jake" we called him. He was a martyr to the vodka.

Once when we were playing at Crans Montana he was in particularly bad shape and arranged for a friend to walk one hole
ahead of him in order to leave a small bottle of vodka beside
the little 150-yard marker bushes that were dotted around
the golf course. After a couple of days of this, a Scottish terror
of a caddie named Blackie got wise to what was happening
and decided to get in on the act. He began following the trail
of vodka. He swapped the vodka for water and got himself as
drunk as a skunk in the process. Jacobs, of course, was frantic
but he could not catch up to his accomplice who was always
a step ahead, diligently doing his duty.

After the round it did not take long for Jake to figure out
who the culprit was who had stolen his vodka. He threatened
all sorts of misfortune on Blackie's person but—in all truth—
he really did not care. Jake hardly cared about anything for
very long. The strange thing is that if Jake *had* drunk all of
that vodka, he would still have finished his round as sober as
he began it. He had amazing capacity. Blackie, on the other
hand, was out of his tree.

******

We were at Epsom RAC one time on a scorching, sunny
day. All the caddies were sitting around the fountain in front
of the clubhouse trying to keep cool and waiting for our players to return from the practise ground. Giant, decorative
goldfish populated the water. Vincent Cronin, who was Liam
Higgins's caddie at the time, was a keen fisherman. No matter
how warm it was, Vincent always wore a cap that was
adorned with hundreds of colourful fly-fishing hooks. Out of
boredom (or maybe because he was affected by the heat), he
removed one of the hooks from his hat and began gaffing the
goldfish. Of course, he immediately put the startled fish
back into the water without harming them any further, being
content to show off his dexterity. Faldo's caddie at the time

was a precise, prickly Englishman named John Moorehouse. Because of his player's recent successes, John thought he was better than everybody else was and he made a remark that upset Vincent.

"You Irish are all the same: only a crowd of messers [tricksters]."

Vincent did not take the remark well. He lunged at Moorehouse and began shouting while prodding him forcefully with a finger. This frightened the Englishman so much that he jumped backward and tumbled into the fountain. Now *that* most certainly terrorised the goldfish a lot more than any of Vincent's previous antics had done. Moorehouse was destroyed. Dripping wet from head to toe, he struggled out of the water only to hear at that precise moment Faldo's name being announced at the first tee.

With no time to change his wet clothes, Moorehouse had to go straight over and take up his duties. Off down the first fairway he went with one of the locker room attendants attempting to towel him down as they walked. It really was quite a sight, and the stern and impeccably turned out Faldo was far from pleased. Moorehouse was lucky it was such a warm and sunny day. Otherwise, he would have caught pneumonia.

******

Scotty Gilmour and I were asked to drive Tony Jacklin's Rolls Royce Silver Shadow to Wentworth one day. When we were going up the hill at Virginia Water within a few hundred yards of our destination, we ran out of petrol. Fortunately, there was a garage nearby and we chugged and sputtered our way into the forecourt. The pump attendant was delighted when he saw the magnificent machine entering his domain. He may even have had a caddie-like mirage of a tip coming to him. He was brought sharply back to reality, however, when we told him to put £1 worth of petrol into the tank.

There was no way that we were going to subsidise the wealthy Jacklin, but we did not realise that a quid's worth of petrol would barely get us to the VIP car park at the golf club—if we were lucky.

Later that day, no sooner had Tony started the engine than the tank ran dry once more. He had to send out for a can of fuel in order to get him out to the same petrol station that we had been in earlier. I am sure the pump attendant was totally confused by all of the comings and goings. I don't need to tell you that we were never trusted with the care of the Silver Shadow again.

More Caddie Yarns

******

One of the most colourful of the many Irish caddies I met over the years was Paddy Mooney. Paddy was attached to Elm Park and used to work for David Jones from Bangor. He always wore a flat cap. I never saw him without it, rain or shine, indoors or outdoors. He was fairly unusual among the caddie fraternity because he never smoked or drank. However, he was always scheming to put himself in place for a dropsy [tip], that most beloved of every caddie's desires. Paddy's favourite ruse was to go Greyhound Racing in the evening after the golf because he would very likely meet some of the golfers there. Although he would never place a bet himself, he would hang around the bookie stalls all evening. Whenever he saw somebody he knew, he would approach and give them—even if they didn't ask for it—a guaranteed tip on the next race.

"I have a hot one straight from the stables that number (whatever) is a certainty," he'd whisper under his breath.

He would then proceed to give six different tips to six different people. One was sure to win and Paddy would be in the right place to receive his dropsy or gratuity from the grateful client when they returned to collect their winnings.

Smythie comprehensively defeated David Jones in the final of the Carroll's Match-Play Tournament at Connemara in 1980 and my favourite memory of Mooney was that he was so disgusted that I had gotten the better of him in our harmless little side-wager that he took off his cherished cap and kicked it along the ground all the way back to the club-house.

******

The vast majority of caddies and players love to have a flutter on golf and football, but they mostly bet on the horses. It gives them an interest while they are waiting for the next round or next flight to the next tournament. I may have spent more time waiting at London's Heathrow Airport than anywhere. I was such a familiar figure there, in fact, that I was on a first-name basis with many of the people who worked there—the cleaners, shop assistants, bar staff, even airline executives. They all knew the golfers and us caddies because we were always on the go. Also automatic (no matter where we were going) was that we would be upgraded to first class. It made the long-haul travelling a lot more comfortable and tolerable. Unfortunately, however, nobody has yet been able to eliminate the waiting. What a pain that is.

I hung around Heathrow so often over the years that I managed to meet many of the top Irish sportsmen in the middle of their own comings and goings. One day I was sitting at the departure gate minding Smythie's gear when Michael Kinane, the champion jockey, came along and sat down beside me.

"Johnny, I want to tell you that I was riding a horse at gallops this morning and it is one of the fastest things I ever sat on!"

The name of the horse was "Generous" and he was rated as Henry Cecil's second-string entry for the Epsom Derby a couple of weeks later. As soon as I got home, I went to Paddy

Power's bookie shop and had "a good cut" at 14/1. Once I had got my own bet on, I told everybody I knew, including all the players and caddies. By the time the horse got to the starting gate the odds were down to 8/1.

The Derby is always run on a Wednesday, which is pro-am day on the golf circuit. That particular Wednesday there was a strangely giddy atmosphere of expectancy about. I can remember Sam Torrance rubbing his hands with glee as he waited for news of the result of the race to filter through on one of the many small transistor radios that were being listened to surreptitiously all around the golf course. Suddenly there was a huge cheer; it was as if England had scored the winning goal in the World Cup final at Wembley. Kinane and Generous had done it! I was the toast of the clubhouse when I got in. The champagne flowed that evening. It seemed as if everybody had a few bob on the winner and the bookies got one hell of a pasting.

******

One of the best places in the world to caddie (let alone play golf) is at Sunningdale, near London, England. They certainly have the right approach to golf at that famous old club. Darren Clarke and Paul McGinley are both members and the best part of going around with them is when we reach the wooden halfway hut that is situated in the middle of the two golf courses called, rather originally, "The Old" and "The New." Behind the ninth green on the New and the tenth green on the Old, steward-cum-restaurateur Vernon Collinson, serves up what could only be described as "gourmet golf food." The best part of this particular pit stop is that the caddies are always served first! Vernon's staff members provide piping hot tea, chocolate, or coffee in enormous enamel mugs. However, if one of the members happens to have his dog along, the four-legged one will get precedence over everybody—including the caddies. It is a delightful, topsy-turvy world at Sunningdale. If you happen to be Darren Clarke's caddie you might have to hang around and allow a couple of groups to go through while the big guy "destroys" at least half a dozen of the biggest, juiciest, meatiest sausages you ever did see! The more health-conscious McGinley is likely to have a lonesome smoked salmon or perhaps a Brie and cranberry sandwich. It sure as hell beats those ghastly hot dogs and Gatorade that are served in the halfway huts in the U.S.

The Holmpatrick Cup

"Is there any chance that you might do me a big favour?" says I to the greatest goalkeeper in the history of soccer: Pat Jennings of Tottenham Hotspur, Arsenal, and Northern Ireland.

"Sure, Reilly. Just ask."

"Could you send me a football autographed by as many of the top players in England as you possibly can, so that I can raffle it at a charity day that I am organising to raise funds for the blind?"

"No problem," Pat replied, and there wasn't, either, with him or any of the other top sports personalities that I requisitioned in various ways. Everybody I asked to help me was delighted to be able to demonstrate their appreciation of their own good fortune in life by showing solidarity with those less fortunate than themselves. Pat Jennings sent the football in plenty of time. A few weeks later, it arrived at Spawell Golf Centre marked for my attention. That item alone raised £5,000. My Jersey friend Jerry Mynes bought it (probably as an act of atonement for all of his evil deeds against me over

Seve had plenty of help in lining up this putt while blindfolded at my outing for the blind.

the years). Actually, I'm sure he wanted to make a significant contribution toward the huge cost of training a guide dog. His was one of many similar gestures by some great friends of mine. For example, three anonymous members of the K-Club gave me an envelope with a similar sum. They're only wish was that their names not be mentioned publicly.

"Just throw it in the kitty," I was told.

I networked like mad in those days after being inspired spontaneously and "out of the blue" at my local watering hole, the Spawell. It happened on a dull, damp, cold winter morning. I was reading the newspaper and having a coffee, basically minding my own business, when I casually looked out the window of the clubhouse and saw some fairly strange happenings on the golf course. I couldn't figure it out. I called over to Paul Anderson, one of the barmen, and asked him to explain it all.

"Oh, that is just the Blind Golfers' Society having an outing," he said. "Aren't they great?"

They most certainly were, as were the fellows who were with them—Jimmy Murray and Tony Hayes—acting as their "eyes." Those guys had to put the players in position over the ball, aim them, and tell the players how far they had to hit it. *They're real caddies,* I thought to myself. I was impressed. I was even more impressed when the group came into the bar when they had finished their game. The group, which included Paddy Coyle, Owen Kyne, Willam Roode, John Fennelly, Sam McMahon, Des Doyle, Paul O'Rahilly, Seamus Ryan, Frank McDougall, Martina Lowe, and May Dwyer turned out to be a fun-loving bunch with a marvellously positive outlook on life. When I heard that it cost £15,000 to train a single guide dog and that there was no money forthcoming from our stingy national government, I became rather emotional about it. Right then and there, I resolved to find a way to help the society raise some badly needed funds.

Almost immediately I began to enlist the help and support of every golfer and celebrity that I had met at pro-ams over the years. I asked everybody if they would help me by giving me cash donations or items as prizes for an auction. Everyone responded magnificently.

The owners of the Spawell Golf and Leisure Centre kindly donated the use of their facilities for free, and then received the shock of their lives when some of the top European Tour players—who were competing in the European Open at the K-Club—turned up to play in a three-hole competition. What made this event so different was the fact that everybody played *blindfolded.* I can assure you that it was a pretty unique and humbling experience for everyone concerned. The pros had no idea what they were letting themselves in for when they agreed to come along. Paul McGinley and Padraig Harrington had some warning in advance and they sneaked in a bit of secret practise (not that it did them much good). It took some courage and humility on the professional's part to allow themselves to look foolish in public. But the likes of Sergio Garcia, Bernhard Langer, Thomas Bjorn, Seve Ballesteros, and all the other famous players who turned up did not bother about such trifles. And I will always be grateful to them.

I ran the event for four years in a row and thousands of spectators always came out to watch the stars. Seve was clearly the crowd favourite and the biggest drawing card and boy, did he ham it up! Every single one of the pros who played told me how surprised they were to learn that playing blindfolded was so difficult. Not being able to see the ball or the target was not the only problem; there were also problems with rhythm and balance. In the end, we managed to collect over £100,000 and it was enough to train seven guide dogs. Not too surprisingly, the clinically blind golfers were much too good for those with blindfolds on and they were victorious every time, which made the occasion more enjoyable and memorable for them.

In 1998, much to my surprise, I was voted "Dublin Citizen of the Month" for January on account of the success of the event. However, I did enjoy being invited to the Mansion House by the Lord Mayor for a big night out.

In a quite subconscious way, I think the reason why I became so passionate about helping the Society of the Blind went back to 1969 when I joined Carlow Golf Club as an "out of town" member. Carlow is a fine heathland golf course about 50 miles south of Dublin. Christy O'Connor Jr. was only beginning his successful tournament-playing career at the time, so to help supplement his income he was the resident club professional at Carlow. When the club decided to look for new members, Christy told me about it and helped in having my application accepted. The morning I turned up for my first game, Christy acted as matchmaker and fixed me up to play in a tournament with a fellow I did not know. The tourney was called the Holmpatrick Cup. Every year this competition is played at golf clubs all over Ireland. The winners of the better-ball format then go forward to play in a national final later in the year. The proceeds from the entry fees at all of the participating clubs are donated to the Society for the Blind.

Anyway, I arrived at Carlow Golf Club for my very first game as a member, not knowing the protocol or that a tournament had been scheduled for the same day. I went into Christy Jr.'s small shop to say "Hello" and to find out if, and when, I could have a tee-time. He welcomed me and told me that there was another new member, Denis White, looking for a partner to play with him in the competition. After Christy introduced us, we agreed to team up. I had already submitted my Artisan's handicap for approval and the club certified a rather generous 14.

I knew the course well, having being around it several times previously. My putter really enjoyed the greens that day. I putted the lights out and then on top of that, I holed out two approaches from the fairway at Nos. 10 and 13 for a pair of eagle twos! My personal gross score of 72 shots ensured that I hardly needed a partner but Denis White made a few telling contributions of his own and we romped home. Not surprisingly, there was a "steward's enquiry" into my handicap, but everything was found to be in order. I certainly did not do anything illegal (holing two shots from the fairway was simply luck). Subsequently, the handicap committee cut me to a 10 handicap and that clipped my wings forever. The 72 was a fluke. I never contended in a tournament at Carlow again.

Later that year when Denis and I went to Milltown for the national final, it was my proudest day as a golfer. My mother Julia, who had never set foot on a golf course before, came to watch me play. My dad unfortunately would not come because he refused to request leave from his army duties. If it had been on his day off, he said he might have turned up. But his attitude was still quite dismissive.

Now I must say I have mixed feelings about Milltown Golf Club because a member of the staff ejected me from the clubhouse on another occasion when I was there. It was for the crime of being "only a caddie and not allowed in here." Earlier that day I had been caddying for the husband and wife team of John and Imelda Gleeson. Both are good golfers and prominent members of the club. In fact, I was more than just a caddie to the Gleesons because I was also their "odd job" man and a kind of property "adviser." They were severely embarrassed that I had been treated this way and did not know what to do. However, I was promptly reinstated by the club captain, Joe Fanagan when he was made aware of what had happened.

"Please come back in, Reilly," he said. He invited the Gleesons and me to join him at the captain's table. I greatly appreciated that. Joe Fanagan, by the way, is a man so steeped in golf that he has the rare distinction of fathering a Walker Cup player (Jody) and a Curtis Cup player (Susan).

At Milltown, I reverted to my original 14 handicap, just for the day. That gave me back my competitive edge and Denis and I were victorious once again. My mother often remarked that golf was "a silly game," but she was thrilled when her son helped beat the rest of Ireland. I gave her the perpetual trophy and replica to bring home. The replica had a place of honor on her mantlepiece until the day she died.

Kiawah Island

"Do you realise that you were doing 75 in a 55-mile-an-hour zone?" asked the menacing Mike Tyson look-alike in a policeman's uniform.

In my best and most beguiling brogue, I replied, "No, Officer. I was looking at those signs along the road that say "75.""

"That is the number of the *highway*," he said, "not the speed limit. Interstate 75."

"Oh my God!" says I, acting surprised and emphasising my accent.

"May I please see your driver's licence, sir?"

It was in a bag in the trunk so I went back there and rooted around for it. While searching, I had another typical Reilly brainwave: Irish driving licences are bilingual! I opened the page that was printed in Irish and handed it to the patrol officer.

"What kind of writing is this? Where y'all from?"

"Ireland, sir. We are golf caddies, here for the World Cup in South Carolina next week. And, sir, we are lost."

"You're Irish?" asks the Officer, brightening up considerably. He was black as the ace of spades. "My folks come from Galway."

"That's where we're from!" says I, getting the message and seeing a way out of the fine mess we were in. "Galway is our hometown. Have you ever been there, Officer?"

"You Irish," he said, shaking his head, "are unbelievable. Only an Irishman could think that quickly. Look, I cannot be bothered trying to write those weird letters in my book. They're worse than Russian, man. Go on, get out of my sight and be careful how y'all drive now. Ya heah?"

We had travelled across the Atlantic two weeks before the 1997 World Cup because many of the European players were involved in the Sarazen World Open at Stone Mountain, Georgia. We then had a week off and flying back home was not a viable option. It was far cheaper and more sensible to stay in America. Padraig and Caroline had decided to take off on their own somewhere, so some other caddies and I had decided to hire a car and drive down to Florida for a bit of a holiday. My companions included David "Magic" Johnson, Darren "The Kid" Reynolds, Alan "Spider" Kelly, and a Spanish kid, Domingo.

We set off early on Sunday morning and headed for Jacksonville. For once I allowed Kelly to do the driving. Big mistake. Another one I made was to get into the back seat and fall fast asleep. I did not keep an eye on things as I normally would. When I woke up I quickly saw road signs referring to "Pensacola" and knew straightaway that we were on the wrong side of the state. In Irish terms, it was like being in the wrong country. That's how big Florida is in comparison. Reluctantly, Kelly allowed me to take over the driving.

We were a hundred miles or so out of our way, so I pressed the metal and headed back east at a fair ol' clip. The inevitable happened: a police car appeared out of nowhere and we were signalled to pull over. We were then told to get out, put our hands on the roof of the car and spread our legs—just like you would see in the movies. I could not really blame the officers for treating us like that because we were in a bit of a state due to the heat and we were not looking our respectable best. It was fortunate for us that it was Sunday because we were all suffering badly from the drought and unable to buy beer anywhere. We would have been in much deeper trouble if that had been the case. Luckily, we were soon allowed to be on our way once more. We headed down the road breathing sighs of relief all round.

Some bright spark in our hotel at the Sarazen Open told us that he had prebooked us into "The Red Roof Inn" in Jacksonville. He said we would have no trouble finding it. But when we got to Jacksonville the place was as big as Dublin and there seemed to be hundreds of hotels with red roofs. It was all too much for us. We gave up looking for our lodgings and decided to rest our bones in a more-than-adequate downtown Days Inn instead. Because of the long journey in the heat and humidity, we were all gasping for a beer and some food. After freshening up a bit, we walked down the street to this lively place—completely unknown to us—called Hooters. It featured scantily dressed young waitresses parading their assets. The younger guys thought they had died and gone to heaven and would have happily stayed there for breakfast, lunch, and dinner. I had seen all that stuff before and did not allow it to deflect me from my primary goal of enjoying a long, cool drink. Unfortunately, Darren looked even younger than his tender years and he was asked for his ID. That tore it. He was under 21; he was refused service and asked to leave.

Janey, will I ever get a drink? I thought to myself, beginning to feel more frantic by the minute. We spilled out onto the street once more, mumbling and grumbling. Then out of the blue I heard a voice say:

"Is that you, Reilly?"

I wheeled around, surprised to hear a friendly voice. It belonged to none other than an old friend from Dublin, Joe

Graham, who was standing right behind me accompanied by his wife, Gaye.

"Holy smoke! Joe, you sure pop up in the most unexpected places," says I.

Joe and Gaye immediately took charge of all our needs. They directed us down the street to a fabulous Italian restaurant where we were able to eat and drink to our heart's content. Then they took us back to their apartment where we had more drinks and a good old Irish singsong. The next day they took us on a guided tour of the northeast coast of Florida. We visited Amelia Island, St. Augustine, and Ponce de Leon Inlet Lighthouse, all places steeped in American history dating back to the 1780s. They were superb tour guides and we all had a wonderful time.

The following day the Grahams took us to a Safari and Wildlife Park. I was fascinated by the alligators that were lying at the edge of a small lake with only a two-foot-tall wall separating them from a very tasty public. What really intrigued me though, and had me scratching my head in wonder, was a big sign in red letters beside the lake. It read:
"DANGER! SWIMMING PROHIBITED."
I am still trying to figure out who would want to go swimming with the alligators?

As soon as our Florida holiday was over, we headed up to South Carolina, where I was about to become involved in the most exciting triumph of my entire caddying career. Ireland, represented by Padraig Harrington, and Paul McGinley won the World Cup at the notorious Ocean Course at Kiawah Island Resort. As a proud Irishman, it was a special feeling to think that I had played a small part in bringing about that victory. Also memorable, however, was the unheralded behind-the-scenes ingenuity that I had to come up with in order to get to that rather irritatingly inaccessible course each day.

As the Americans might say, Kiawah Island is out in the

"boondocks." It's in the middle of an alligator- and snake-infested, saltwater swamp, about 10 miles from Charleston, South Carolina. Because we had returned the rental car that we had taken to Florida and did not want the expense of hiring another one, we found ourselves having a difficult time obtaining transportation to and from the golf course. We grew tired of the problem very quickly, especially since the players were having no such difficulty.

After a couple of days I thought, *Enough of this nonsense.* I then began to observe the procedure that the players used to obtain a courtesy car.

Presenting myself as bold as brass in front of the man who was dispensing the vehicles, I said, "I'd like a courtesy car, please."

"Who are you?" he asked.

"I am the coach of the Irish team," says I, exaggerating my position in the pecking order just a bit.

"No problem, sir," he said.

It turned out that the courtesy cars were actually police patrol vehicles and they came with driver attached. For insurance purposes, I presume. So now, not only did I have my own car, but I had a chauffeur at my beck and call as well. I loaded the car up with my grateful caddie colleagues and asked the driver to take us back to our apartment in Charleston. On the way, I asked the driver where the best place would be to get some food and drink later that evening.

"What time do you want me to pick you up, Sir?" says our chauffeur.

"That would be very nice of you," I said. "About 7 o'clock, please."

"I will collect you then, sir."

I thought to myself: *Why is he calling me "Sir?"* After all, we were in America, the greatest republic of them all. Anyhow, the chauffeur shows up on time and he takes us about 10 miles away to a high-class restaurant that had an Irish pub attached. The whole staff seemed to have relatives in Ireland;

they made us as welcome as the flowers in May, and could not have looked after us any better. There were fellows coming at us from all angles buying us free drinks. It was a caddie's paradise! At one juncture I asked our ever-so- efficient driver if he would like to join us.

"No, thank you, sir," he replied. "I can't drink while on duty. But just tell me when y'all'd like to go back to your apartment and I'll be here."

"Ten o'clock would be nice," says I, getting to like this arrangement more and more by the minute and wishing that we could take both car and driver back to Ireland with us at the end of the week. From then on, everything went like clockwork. It did not take Harrington and McGinley long to figure out what was going on. They were amused but warned me that if I was rumbled, they didn't want any part of it!

One evening we all left in a convoy. Harrington and his missus were in one car, McGinley and his caddie Alan Kelly in another, and myself, David, Domingo, and Darren in the third one. One of the police drivers was a keen golfer and he had pestered us to be allowed to examine the golf clubs belonging to the Irish team. We said that we would do it back at the apartment where a few photographs of the drivers and the entire Irish group could also be taken.

Later that evening the three patrol cars swept into the courtyard of the apartment complex with only that in mind. But as we came through the gate, I could see pandemonium ahead of me—bodies ducking and diving in all directions. There must have been an illicit drug party or some other skulduggery going on. Our policeman friends, however, pretended not to see anything (which was impossible) and carried on as if everything were normal. Nothing was about to divert them from their declared mission of inspecting our players' golf clubs.

As the week went by, I gradually became cocksure of myself as a result of being ferried around like a celebrity by my driver. During one of those interminable daily holdups on

the causeway, a traffic policeman stuck his head in through
an open window and asked for an autograph.

"What country do you guys represent?" he asked with a smile.
Quick as flash, I said, "Tir na nOg."

That stunned him into silence and he butted out as quickly
as he had butted in. I then explained to the driver that Tir na
nOg is a mythical fantasyland that exists in Irish folklore, a
place where no one grows old. He got a kick out of that.

I must say that the week's festivities at Kiawah were second to none. There was a fabulous pretournament pro-am
and party at which we met some wonderful people who really
treated us well. Their names are firmly etched in my memory
forever: Dewey Dupont, Bob and Kristi Rummel, Tracey
Fletcher, Scott Boyd, and Scooter Laufer. Unfortunately,
however, I mislaid their addresses so I have not been able to
remain in touch with them.

As the week at Kiawah progressed, our adventures managed to keep getting better and better. Padraig and Paul were
at the top of their games and were in the lead, or near it,
from start to finish. As we turned for home to face the final
nine holes on the last day, we were four strokes in front of
the formidable duo representing the USA: Davis Love and
Freddie Couples. I really had my hands full and was working
overtime helping to keep the Irish lads relaxed and focussed
as the Americans—who were the titleholders and whose rep-
utations need no introduction from me—began to exert
themselves by turning the screws and applying almost
unbearable pressure. They seemed to hit their drives further
and straighter at each succeeding hole. Going up the long
twelfth hole, I was delighted to be able to enlist the assistance of another Irishman, David Feherotti (CBS's Feherty
to you), who was walking along with our group and com-
menting on the play for the television. I asked David to tell
the boys a few jokes to help them to relax. Feherty is a wonderful storyteller. He would be the leading money winner by
a mile in that game. Feherty walked up to an overwrought

McGinley and asked, "What is the most stupid animal in all of creation?"

Paul hadn't a clue, but while he was thinking about it he scored an eagle, which relaxed him so much that he played flawlessly thereafter. Feherty asked Padraig the same question but it did not have the same effect. In fact, Padraig must have thought he was stupid because while he was trying to figure out the answer he played two of the most awful approach shots you ever saw at Nos.14 and 15. Somehow, though, he managed to play miracle recovery shots with his lob wedge each time which saved his bacon. Those two fabulous shots by Harrington took the wind out of Love's and Couples's full sails. The Irish lads were so relaxed from joking with Feherty that it became more like a walk in the park for them. They held on to beat the Americans, and the rest of the world, quite comfortably in the end.

Coming up the last hole, the crowds were going mad. Hundreds of Irish who were on holiday nearby had come along to cheer us home. In America, everyone loves a winner and our drivers were just as thrilled. I need hardly tell you that we celebrated in style that evening. We even visited the hangout of the local police force where half the personnel of Charleston joined us for a joyous knees-up Irish hooley.

All evening long, McGinley and Harrington were still trying to work out the answer to Feherty's riddle. Eventually I put them out of their misery.

"The sardine is the most stupid creature of all," I said. "What other eejit would lock himself into a tin can and leave the key on the outside?"

The lads weren't too impressed with the answer, but I am certain that Feherty's intervention played a major part in the winning of the World Cup of Golf for Ireland.

The next morning, when we arrived at the airport in Atlanta on our way home, a bigwig from "Airport Hospitality" ushered us into the VIP Lounge, where we met Dick Spring, the Irish Foreign Minister and Deputy Prime

Minister. Apparently he had been attending a meeting at the
United Nations. But instead of flying home from New York,
he decided to take a slight detour in order to fly home with
the cup. (Politicians like photo opportunities of that sort, I
guess.) Our next treat was being upgraded to first class.
About 10 other people were "upstairs" with us, returning
home after a family wedding. When they found out who we
were, there was an overwhelming mood of celebration on
that flight for several good reasons. The champagne flowed.
We sang our heads off all the way home to Ireland. It was a
special, never-to-be-repeated experience.

When we arrived at Dublin Airport, you would have
thought that we had won the World Cup of soccer.
Thousands of people were waiting to greet us, and we were
taken straight to the Mansion House in Dublin (not quite
the White House in Washington, D.C. but close to it), where
we were greeted and honoured by the Lord Mayor and members of the government.

A few weeks later, the Lord Mayor hosted a big banquet
for us. There was a spectacular cocktail reception, followed
by a lavish meal that was punctuated with speeches. A presentation was made to the two players and they both spoke
emotionally about their triumph. Quite correctly, they
thanked all the people that had helped them since they were
small kids with stars in their eyes. The Mayor then said that
he had one more presentation to make. We were all wondering what it might be about when I suddenly heard him say
the word "Reilly." It took a few moments to realise that he
was talking about me, and then I heard him say "Head Coach
of the Irish team and the first Irish caddie to win the World
Cup!" I was completely taken aback. Both Padraig and Paul
had been quite generous to me in their speeches, giving me
credit for my contribution, but neither had mentioned my
means of transportation while we were at Kiawah. Obviously,
the word had slipped out and the ears of the Irish media had
begun to flap. In any case, I was presented with a stunningly

beautiful, inscribed Waterford glass crystal fruit bowl. The inscription reads:

To Reilly, the first Irish caddie to win the World Cup of Golf

I was thrilled and I must say that I enjoyed being the centre of attention for an Andy Warhol moment. My picture was in all the newspapers the next morning and the gentlemen of the press asked me for interviews. That win at Kiawah Island is something I will always remember with great pride, and I still have the crystal bowl displayed prominently in my home.

It brings a smile to my face every time I see it.

About the Authors

John O' Reilly began caddying on the European Professional Golf Association Tour in the 1970s and retired in 1999. During that time, he toted golf bags and dispensed sage advice in numerous countries around the world.

In 2000, John was inducted into the Professional Caddies Hall of Fame, one of only a handful to be selected since its inception. John and his partner, Margaret, have six children and they live in Dublin, Ireland.

Ivan Morris is the author of *Only Golf Spoken Here: Colourful Memoirs of a Passionate Irish Golfer*. He is a single-digit player, has participated in numerous local and international amateur tournaments over the past forty years, and is still in search of the perfect round. He and his wife, Marie, have three children and they live in Limerick, Ireland.